MW01515176

Faces

By Philip J. Braun

Copyright © 2006 by Philip J. Braun

ISBN 0-7414-3079-7

Published by:

PUBLISHING.COM

1094 New DeHaven Street, Suite 100
West Conshohocken, PA 19428-2713
Info@buybooksontheweb.com
www.buybooksontheweb.com
Toll-free (877) BUY BOOK
Local Phone (610) 941-9999
Fax (610) 941-9959

Printed in the United States of America
Printed on Recycled Paper
Published May 2006

This book is dedicated to

Frances Gumpper

A lovely lady.

Table of Contents

Foreword

This old German, a resident of Flint, Michigan for 75 of his 85 years, was asked by his oldest son more than a year ago to write about the people that he had known throughout his lifetime. In any community there are those who are saints and sinners, leaders and followers, trusted and not trusted, significant and insignificant. One's life is a tapestry woven with threads from all of the above. My life has been colorful, not to mention extremely pleasurable, because of these individuals.

This book is the result of my son's request, and the reader can decide whether the personalities described were worth the effort. I found the time I spent preparing the book to be interesting and memorable in bringing back those many enjoyable years. I trust the reader will feel the same.

Albert John Koegel

Flint, Michigan

In every community you find leaders. Some of them are dynamic and outspoken, makers of newspaper headlines, not shy for adulation by the public. In my experience, having lived all but 10 of my 85 years in Flint, I have known such people, men and women who you call leaders.

Once in a while comes someone who is quiet, efficient, knowledgeable, not interested in headlines. This kind of person is quite rare and soft-spoken, likes to work behind the scenes and give others the credit for progress made. Such a man is Al Koegel. It has been my privilege to call him a good friend.

His firm, Koegel Meats, is well-known far and wide in the Midwest. Koegel hot dogs are an item in Florida and other southern states. Many of his delicious sausages make their way to Florida and far away places in drink coolers and small refrigerators. I have stayed with people in Florida who proudly feature Koegel hotdogs.

But it is the man that this little book prefers to speak of, and his talents and community-mindedness which deserve the adulation and respect.

It is interesting in my case when I consider my own experience trout fishing, and how my father first taught me on the banks of the Maple River south of Pellston, Michigan. It appears that Al had about the same experience early in life and maintains at least one trip each year to that quiet, shaded stream that begins its life in the springs just east of Cross Village and rambles through the countryside to end up in Burt Lake. I have talked to Al and his favorite stretch of the Maple is the same as mine—the stretch between Brutus bridge and the old Iron bridge to the north. Unfortunately, the stream has become a rich man's plaything and to join the club that controls much of the river now is a money-thing that I regret. I can remember as a boy catching my first brookie in that water and realizing that the fish was to be released, according to my father. That was before "catch and release" was even a slogan.

Al's military experience in the Korean War was interesting. He had been trained as a food service supervisor at Ft. Lee, Virginia. He had the first job in Korea of checking up on mess sergeants, so he felt in many cases he had little to tell them. Then he was transferred to a Combat Engineers Battalion and was put in charge of a PX warehouse. He was held accountable for everything that moved out of that PX, which included many truck loads of beer for the GIs.

I remember well a real problem we had in the late 80s at our church, First Presbyterian Church in downtown Flint. The business administrator passed away and Al was asked to help straighten out the accounting. The accounting software was archaic, and he was finally able to convince the trustees (Al was a trustee himself) that they should put in the same accounting software that they used at his sausage factory. In doing so, progress was made. It was determined that the checking account at the church hadn't been reconciled for over a year. Foul play was suspected. But by Al's service and that of two other good members (Howard Gross and Ralph Whittier), when the bank statements were checked out, every penny was accounted for. This whole process was grueling. Much credit must go to Al.

A very worthwhile venture was when Al headed a drive to raise money for the Children's Museum, which was badly needed in this old rust-belt city. The old IBM building near Kettering University was purchased and then the property was donated to Kettering, with the proviso that there would be a lease to the Museum for only $10 a year.

It was also very pleasing to many in Flint when Al accepted the challenge and ran for Trustee of Mott Community College. His work and his steadiness at board meetings became well known. As a result of it, he was reelected to another long term as a trustee.

Flint needs more Al Koegels. They are very hard to find. Many good people are afraid to run for community positions because of the politics involved and much in-fighting. This is a problem every city has. It is unfortunate.

Philip Jacob Braun

Petoskey, Michigan

A few miles north of Flint along the Flint River there is a little hamlet known as Geneseeville. South and a few miles east of there, a Kiwanis health camp existed on the south side of the river during the late 20s through the 60s. For those many years, the Downtown Kiwanis Club of Flint ran a summer camp for children. The original intent was to take 100 kids who had tuberculosis. The camp was the idea of my father and Dr. Frederick Miner, a well-known physician in Flint.

I can remember as a kid going out there in the spring to help my dad and the Kiwanians when we had what was called "Camp Clean-up." It was an all day deal with a supper at night. I remember my father was always one of the cooks for the evening festivities.

At one time there was a girls dorm, a boys dorm, a kitchen, and a swimming pool. Today only the cement bottom of the swimming pool remains, and to the south on a gentle slope back of where the dorms were is a small bronze statue of my father. The place is now surrounded by woods. The camp was a testament to my father and his love for children, which he displayed all his adult life by the organizations that he supported and sometimes chaired—all of them for children.

My father was born before 1900 by a few years. One of my treasures of him is a little blue book which was published once a month in Petoskey by a printer who was the father of one of the boys that made up my father's "gang" in high school. The blue book had an entry in it one day that simply said, "Nothing happened today." One of the boy members was Art Eldridge who became the Harbor Commissioner of Los Angeles; another, Ray Baker, who became a professor at the U-M in Ann Arbor. He was an author and one of his books was entitled *The Indian Drum*. Today that book is remembered by the old folks of Petoskey. It is a tale, some feel true, of an Indian drum that beats one time for each person lost in shipwrecks on the Great Lakes. The drum is supposed to be in the deep woods somewhere east of Cross Village, north of Harbor Springs.

When I was eight years of age, my father gave me a fly rod, flies, waders, and a small creel. He took me to the iron bridge on the Maple River between Brutus and Pellston, north of Petoskey. I had a fishing license and he taught me how to fly fish and how to tie flies. His favorite was the Male Adams which I used for more than 70 years. Not that one, but others that were tied. By the time I was able to drive a car, I was alone fishing on the Maple each summer. From then on, it was one of my favorite pastimes.

In addition, because of my father's girth and bad legs, we did a lot of float fishing on the AuSable, the PM, and the Manistique.

Sometime in the early 20s, my folks bought a cottage on the south shore of Orrs Point, then known as Long Lake (later renamed Lake Fenton). My mother loved to fish as well as he. Many times the three of us would fish two or three times a week, usually near Ernie Newcombe's diving tower which was right on the edge of the drop-off. We caught bluegills and sunfish, and an occasional black bass. We'd then clean them on shore and put them in a freezer we had in the basement. Then on the weekend we'd have a roast with other cottagers, the fish cooked over charcoal. Bluegills were my favorite.

It was a standing thing for me to have the rowboat ready with a can of worms. My father would be on the dock by 5:30, fresh from his insurance office in Flint. We'd fish for maybe an hour, come in, clean the fish and have supper. One memorable time was on a Sunday when we'd been to a potluck with three other families. Late that day, shortly before dusk, my dad said, "Let's fish for an hour." We got in the boat and took off by Ernie Newcombe's tower. My father sat in the bow of the boat. When it was time to come in (we had a few bluegills) he started to pull up the anchor. With his bulk and the fact that Long Lake had a marl bottom—and the anchor was sucked into that gooey bottom—he proceeded to pull the boat into the water and we were swimming. Those on shore saw us and knew we could easily make the tower. My father was smoking a pipe and had his old fishing hat on, neither of which got wet. The boat went one way, the fish on a stringer another way, and we sat on the deck of the tower. Do you think anyone was going to come and get us? No way. They just sat and roared. Finally, someone had mercy on us and came out. Many times I think of my father, still smoking his pipe with his dry hat and a big smile on his face.

I also remember the time that he had an account, Standard Cotton Products, who made upholstery for GM cars. It was owned by Ellis Warren, a prominent Jewish member of the community. My father was then the Secretary of the new Flint City Club, with headquarters on the sixth floor of the now-defunct Durant Hotel. The City Club had no Jewish members until my father proposed Ellis Warren and indicated that if Warren wasn't elected, they could all go shove it. Ellis Warren became a member.

One thing about my father: his word was his bond. Few questioned his integrity. When he passed away from pneumonia after a three year bout with Parkinson's (in Genesee Memorial Hospital), there was a nice article on the front page of the Journal. At the time, Sally and I were vacationing with her folks in Florida when we got a call that I should fly home because my dad was in a coma. We did. As I held his hand he gripped mine, and died.

Joseph T. Ryder

(1909-1979) Born in Pemberville, Ohio

Prologue

They came from all over that morning. It was a quiet spring day . . . one he would have liked because he was partial to that time of year. In former years when that season of greenness arrived in Michigan you would have found him either up to his favorite stretch of the Black near Vanderbilt where an old gnarled apple tree hung over the clear waters, or you would have seen him with a couple of kids smelling the odors of fresh buckwheat pancakes at the Sugar Bush. He would have been eager and excited about the day ahead.

That spring morning they came from great distances to pay their respects to him. The service was simple as he would have liked. At the close, his eldest son delivered a eulogy that caught the flavor of the man. As they listened, they were caught up in their own reveries of the days they had shared with Joe Ryder.

*   *   *

I had been home from the service just a short while when I had the good fortune to meet Joe Ryder. He had recently been employed by the Mott Foundation to set up the Flint Youth Bureau which later was affiliated with the national Big Brother movement. Its principle aim was to have men work with and counsel boys who did not have a father in the home. Over the course of the next 35 years, in addition to my own involvement in the Big Brother program in which I worked with two different boys, I became a close personal friend of Joe. The same could be said of many other people, not just in Flint, but throughout the country. He was an extraordinary man and the stories about him are legion. A family man, my wife and I had the privilege of spending some wonderful moments with Helen, Joe and their three sons Bob, Bill and Jim.

Joe Ryder loved life. He loved the Sugarbush, where they tapped trees for maple syrup. He loved fishing for perch on Saginaw Bay, and had to be air lifted (with some boys) off the bay one winter day when they were caught on a moving ice pack. For a while after that, his good friends called him "Ice Flow Joe." He also enjoyed the waters of northern Michigan. He was a prolific reader and had a keen interest in the West and the life of the Indian. His modest retreat in the woods between Petoskey and Charlevoix was called *Chanson Du Vent*, which translates into *Song of the Wind*. It became a gathering place for many of his friends where he would regale them with his stories.

One time when Sally and I were there visiting, Joe and I stood on the cliff overlooking Little Traverse Bay and saw 10 or 11 large Mackinac trout float by. Most likely while you were there, he would treat you to his famous cornmeal mush. Sometimes he had a corn roast on the cliff overlooking the bay.

Joe was a doer. He had the ability to bring out the best in people. He could talk with the drifter and the top corporate exec. There were no walks of life he didn't know and understand. He had tremendous drive and creativity. I can remember more than once when in the middle of the night he would be bailing some boy out of jail and working with the courts to try to save that life.

Under his leadership, the Flint Youth Bureau became a model for Big Brothers chapters throughout the nation and Canada. I remember seeing a letter once from Ernest Coulter, the founder of the Big Brother movement. It epitomized Joe's basic philosophy.

> I hope and pray that Big Brothers of America will not permit itself to become involved in too much technique. It does not need that. Rather it needs faith in the inherent goodness and kindness of man, which will develop when wisely encouraged and given a chance to grow. No boy is immune to kindness, personal interest, but it must come from the heart . . . no pretense . . . the youngster is quick to see that. You may know more about ethics, but he knows more about temptation.

Joe Ryder was a problem-solver without getting too involved in theory. Some of his contemporaries in the professional ranks disagreed with some of his methods (I saw this many times). But they never questioned his devotion.

I should explain a little: when Joe found a boy who needed a man to help him, Joe didn't worry about the paperwork (the analysis of the boy, the professional picture of the problem). This could be very useful, but first Joe wanted to get a man, get him started with the boy, and let the paperwork come afterwards.

Those of us who had the privilege to be with and work with Joe Ryder cherish his memory and his tremendous outlook on life.

Now, a few personal memories:

(1) The time that Joe came over to our home on Westwood Parkway and planted two white pines in the back corner of our lot. One grew and is still there growing. The other died. Our son Mark, then only five or six, said, "The one that died. That was Helen." Helen Ryder had passed away perhaps less than a year when Mark made his comment.

(2) A number of us took a fishing trip with Joe each May after Mother's Day when the ice was still on the edges of some of those northern lakes above the Canadian Sault. There was a river by our campsite and Joe said to me one day, "Let's explore it." We took off downstream and had gone perhaps a mile when I, sitting in the bow of the boat, could hear the noise of a small rapids. I said to Joe, "Slow down." We didn't. We were lucky we weren't put under the sod by the waterfall we missed going over.

(3) Whenever he visited you (and this was true with all his friends), if you weren't around, he'd leave a calling card with the drawing of an old hat with an Indian arrow through it. Many of us called him "Injun Joe."

(4) While at Bowling Green, Ohio (just south of Toledo) where he went to college, he set some cross country records that (when I checked a few years ago), were still not beaten.

(5) Joe wouldn't have been possible without Helen. He bailed boys out of jail and took boys on fishing trips at all times. I remember one time when after a trip to Quanacasee, near Bay City on Lake Huron, where everyone was perch fishing, Joe took his head count when they were ready to go back to Flint and one boy was missing. Joe stayed all night looking for him. Finally, Joe was advised that the boy got mixed up and hitch-hiked back to Flint.

C. S. Mott

Flint, Michigan

Industrialist, mayor, round-table member, husband, father, creator of the Mott Foundation which today is one of the largest foundations for good in the country, which has helped thousands of people throughout the world…

To me he was just Mr. Mott. While I was not one of the privileged who called him C.S. or Charlie, I did have more than one occasion to call on him in his later years at his estate, Applewood. I treasured my visits.

One time I took him a picture of Joe Ryder, of whom he was very fond. Another time I visited him to talk about Flint. His wife, Ruth, was one of the finest women I ever knew, and I served on her Applewood Board for many years.

The stories about Mr. Mott are legion and I have one. Sometime in the '60s, the Mott Children's Clinic was dedicated. It stands today next to Hurley Medical Center. Mr. Mott brought down from the Upper Peninsula one selfless doctor, Art Tuuri, to run the clinic. The dedication was a Chamber of Commerce affair, and I was the M.C.

We were seated at circular tables for lunch that day. I was at the same table with Mr. Mott, Dr. Tuuri, George Hall, and others. It happened to be during the Christmas season. George Hall was the manager of Sears and Mr. Mott still owned and operated Smith Bridgman's, a large department store centrally located downtown. As we sat there that day at lunch, George leaned over toward Mr. Mott and I heard him say, "C.S., you'll get a kick out of this. Today we had a would-be shoplifter at Sears. When that happens, we take the suspect into my office and my secretary categorizes and lists by price every item before we call the police. You'll be interested to know that of the $96 worth of merchandise, only $18 came from my store, Sears. The rest came from your store, Smith Bridgman's." Mr. Mott took a look at George, smiled, and said quickly, "That's the proper proportion, George." At that time he had to be in his late 80s and what a quick, rapier-like response. Everyone who heard it was delighted.

The other story I like to tell is not one that I witnessed, but was told to me by George Spaulding years ago when he was the general manager at Applegate Chevrolet. One day George delivered a new Chevrolet to C.S. Mott. The car had come in from the factory. The paperwork indicated it was at dealer cost, because Mr. Mott was a Director of General Motors. George took the paperwork to Mr. Mott in the Mott Foundation Building for his signature. He looked at the amount and said, "On the dealer-installed heater you only gave me a 25% discount. As a Director, I am entitled to 40% off." George agreed, went back to the dealership, had the papers retyped and took them back for Mr. Mott's signature. Mr. Mott never even checked the figures that time, merely signed them and returned them to George with a smile and a handshake. Mr. Mott saved $12—this is the same man who back then gave $127 million to the Flint Schools.

The other personal story is about my folks. Each winter in their later years they would take the train to Tucson, Arizona and stay for a month at the Pioneer Hotel. Each year when they entered their rooms for the first time, there would be an arrangement of flowers from C.S. Mott.

E. Paul Lynch

Flint, Michigan

Better known to his many friends as *Deke*, I first knew him when I was a late teenager when he came over with his wife, Millie, and her mother, known as Gramma Kramer. This was when we were first living on 1618 Linwood off E. Court Street in the Central High district. I had convinced the Superintendent of Schools, Lee Lamb, that I should stay at Northern to finish out my senior year. To do so, I had to get up at 5:30, shower, dress, and walk the mile to Central across the field where Mott Community College now stands. Then I went around the athletic field, walked between Whittier Junior High and Central to get on a 6:30 bus to downtown. In those days the connections on E. Court Street weren't good enough. When I got downtown, I had to transfer, then wait to get off on N. Saginaw Street at Leith, and walk six more blocks to Northern. Today, all the kids would have cars and wouldn't think of doing what I had to do to satisfy my ego that "to go to Central was like eating dog food for breakfast."

Deke was a powerful man, and my father and he tried to try to eat each other under the table. Deke usually won. At that time, I didn't know that he had played end for the old Columbus, Ohio Tiger football team which was one of the teams that was a forerunner of the National Football Association. He told me one time when I got to know him better that one day in a game, he had to tackle "Fats" Henry coming toward him with the ball, or Fats would score for his team. Fats laid a hand on Deke and he found himself in the mud of the field as Fats went on to score.

It was here in 1927, after graduating from Ohio Northern, that he married Millie, who was a great athlete herself. When they came to Flint for Deke to work at Buick, Millie played basketball as a forward in a league along with Jennie Weiss (of golf fame at the Flint Club). Deke played on a basketball team organized by Buick along with Reese Jones, Mel Winer, and a host of well known Flint athletes.

One thing I remember about Deke was that he had a host of friends from every walk of life. He gave each of them a nickname: Art Crawley, the manager of Consumers Powers was Leroy; Bert Beveridge, one of the owners of Automobile Carriers, was Cozy because of all the cozy deals he made with GM to haul new cars; my dad was known as Bull and I was known as Little Bull.

During the war when I was overseas, Deke, Millie, Gramma Kramer, my dad and my mother had a big victory garden in the back of Linwood. One day, my father gave Millie the business. It seemed that while my folks were on a vacation to Arizona, Millie took some of the rocks and whitewashed them. When my dad saw them he said to her, "You could have better used your time taking weeds out of the garden." Today Millie is 103 years old and going strong. Deke passed away sometime ago. Even in her 70s, Millie was an ice skater, and a beautiful one at that. She skated many times at Ballenger Park with many people looking on at her.

Along with my father, Deke was co-chairman of the Kiwanis Club Health Camp started by Dr. Miner and my dad. At some point in time, Deke was made the head of the United Way of Genesee County. With his wide range of friends, it was a blessing for Flint. If I have the story straight, it was Deke who first approached the unions and sold them on the importance of the United Way to the community. He asked them to consider monthly payroll deduction from the workers, with the money going to the United Way.

My last memory of Deke is one day at the old YMCA on Kearsley Street, across from the Palace Theatre. I was showering and so was Deke. We had our lockers next to each other. When it got time to get dressed, I couldn't help but laugh at Deke's procedure: first he put on an old hat, then all his clothes over it. How he did it, I can't figure.

Doris (Logeman) Rich

Washington, D.C.

I was very pleased a few years ago to pick up the evening paper and read about Doris. My wife of 58 years, Sally Cummings, and I had been good friends with both Doris and her brother, Henry, in Flint Junior College. Our paths had crossed through the years and we were on hand when both Doris and Henry had been given the Flint Central High Alumni Award.

The article about Doris was taken from the New York Times and it concerned itself with the great biography that she published about Amelia Earhart, the flier. Since that book, which was on the *New York Times* non-fiction bestseller list for some time, she has recently finished a biography on Jacquelyn Cochran, another fine aviatrix, and hopes to get it published.

Doris was a great leader at JC, a kind of bon vivant, a willing counselor to all the girls. With a pack of cigarettes and the latest word on how to "get your man," she became very popular. I remember a time after World War II when she and her husband Stan Rich, came to Flint to visit and they stayed at the then-Flint Tavern Hotel, across from the Durant. A big party ensued with all of Doris's girl friends, and I distinctly remember a bathtub loaded with gin.

Doris's career has been exceptional. From an article in the *Tempo* magazine, I see some parallels in the lives of Doris and America Earhart. It said,

> By the time she took her final, fatal flight in 1937, Amelia Earhart was caught in the vortex of two converging currents–pride and money. Her reputation for honesty, commitment, and courage was at stake. So was her livelihood. With almost all of her capital invested and her future earnings pegged to a successful flight, her husband, George Palmer Putnam, had already booked her into at least 70 post-flight lectures at $500 each. She had to circumnavigate the globe.

Both Earhart and Doris were tomboys at home. Both volunteered to help soldiers (different wars) and both had a desire to defy stereotypical roles for women. Doris liked the way Earhart wore slacks, and she was known to have said, "It's my theory that Amelia Earhart, Kate

Hepburn, and Marlene Dietrich made it acceptable to wear them on the streets and at informal social gatherings."

Doris joined the American Red Cross in World War II. After that, she had a tour in Korea, where she taught Marines how to transform scrap metal into jewelry. There she met Stan Rich, a bureau chief for United Press. She at the time was a public information officer for the U.S. Army headquartered in Seoul, Korea. After a six-week courtship and a two month honeymoon in New York, they hopped on a freighter to Shanghai. As Doris said to me, "It took us 60 days to travel from New York through the Panama Canal and the hit song that year was "On a Slow Boat to China." While in an incredibly cheap hotel in Shanghai for two months, they witnessed the execution of three black market dealers by the Nationalist police and they were sick to their stomachs at the sight. Shanghai was a city where 11 year old girls in bamboo cages were being sold for prostitution.

With only $18 in their pockets, they traveled to Hong Kong where Stanley became associate editor of an English language newspaper. While there, they got lucky and won $5,000 in a sweepstakes. Two children were born in the Far East and Doris taught English and civics and private schools. Their experiences were just beginning.

Stan served in Vietnam in '66-67 with the U.S. Information Agency followed by eight months in Washington, D.C. in intensive training of the Chinese language by the State Department. From there they were off again to Bangladesh where Doris taught English to student nurses at a Catholic hospital. In '68-71, Stan was the radio correspondent from Burma to Australia for the Voice of America and from '72-78, the chief of the Thai section of the Voice of America in Washington, D.C. Doris, not to be outdone by her traveling husband, got her Bachelor degree in East Asian studies. Then, on the road again as the song says, Stan served as Public Affairs officer in Thailand while Doris kept busy (real busy) feeding children of Cambodian refugees near the Thai-Cambodian border.

Finally, yes finally if you are still with me, they returned to Washington in '83, and Doris started working on the biography of Earhart. In order to do it right in the period of research, she managed to take 13 trips across the country, combing archives.

All in all, she is a great gal with many rich experiences and has lectured extensively. Oh yes, they raised three children.

Keith Norwalk

Grand Rapids, Michigan

Keith's dad was the principal at old Flint Northern while I was there in 1936, '37, and '38. Somehow early in that time, Keith and I found out that we shared a mutual interest in fly fishing, he being taught by his father, and I by mine.

The old homestead where Keith had been born and where his father, Otto Norwalk had lived as a boy, was in a farm house up on the hill just south of Beulah, in the hamlet of Benzonia.

One spring day in May of 1938 before we graduated from Northern, Keith invited me to be his guest at his folks' home there, and we went up late on Friday. That Saturday morning—early in the morning—we fished the Betsie, which runs into Lake Michigan at Frankfurt. We were lucky to catch a couple of nice browns with a fly I hadn't heard of at the time, a Mickey Finn. It acted like a minnow as it skirted across the water of the Betsie. Since salmon were planted in Lake Michigan, in the spring today the big salmon have taken over the little stream.

After fishing and quitting for lunch at the farm, Keith suggested that we should take Otto's Model T and try to get up as far as the village of Empire (36 miles away). While we were at it, maybe we could try to get up on Sleeping Bear Dunes with the car. I was game.

Arriving at Empire which is just a few miles south of the big dunes, we took a trail to the north. After a while, it became very tough to navigate and we proceeded to sink the front end of the Model T deep in the sand. Keith got out with a shovel and started to dig while I tried to move the car with both the front and rear bands in the band box. It wasn't too long before I had stripped the front band and all we had left was the back band. Then I dug for a while and Keith worked on the back band. Finally, we were able to get the wheels out and then had the daunting task of backing up 36 miles to Benzonia. This took us back through Empire with all the dogs in town yelping and astonished townsfolk looking on and laughing at a couple of 18 year old kids.

We made the main road and started down it backwards at the brisk pace of about six or seven miles an hour, the afternoon turning toward night. At some point Keith said to me, as cars passed us and people thought we were crazy, "I've lost my watch. I must have dropped it while we were digging."

About two miles down the main highway, with amazed and laughing motorists, a State Police patrol car appeared and pulled us over. After listening to his ire, we told him what our problem was and that all we had was the rear band. So, with that, he turned on his siren and began to give us an escort for 34 miles. After what seemed like hours later, with dusk settling, we arrived in the town of Beulah. We were greeted by half of the town who had heard about a couple of crazy kids going backwards.

Now ahead lay the challenge. Benzonia is up on the hill and the grade is eight, and it's a mile climb. If the band didn't hold, we would slide back into Beulah and Crystal Lake. But, by sheer perseverance and luck we made it, with the trooper sounding his siren and leading us into Otto Norwalk's back yard. Here is where the story should end, but it didn't.

About 55 years later at about 10:00 in the evening as Sally and I headed for a good night's sleep, the phone rang. A voice said to me, without any "Hello" first, "Phil, I got my watch back." I recognized Keith's voice coming from Grand Rapids, and I said, "What watch?" Over the years, I had forgotten about the watch.

Keith went on to say, "Don't you remember back in '38, when we dug out Old Betsy above Empire?" Then I remembered. Then he said, "A couple from Farmington Hills were hiking on that trail and the sun glinted on the watch after all these years. They picked it up and when they turned it over, it showed my name and Flint Northern High School and the date that we had won the Class A Debate title from Benton Harbor. They called Northern, got a clerk in the office, and when they explained their problem, the clerk found a computerized copy of the list of all graduates from Northern. They looked up the Class of '38, found my address, and I have my watch."

I also remember when Keith and I were at the old Flint Junior College, we pulled a prank. At the time we *enjoyed every minute of it.* One wintry night at his house we made a dummy, hat and all, and we took it downtown to the Flint River bridge by Albert Schiapiccase's candy store. We got around in the back and put the dummy in the river in such a way that you could see it and it looked like a body caught in the debris. Then we stood on the bridge about 10:00 at night and waited for someone to walk by. Along came an old drunk and we pointed out the body in the river. That's all he needed. He ran screaming and must have alerted the police and the river squad. We watched as the river boat got into the current and picked up the body (dummy with the hat). Oh, to be young again.

James Baker

Flint Junior College ('39-'40)

In the fall of '39, I entered the Flint Junior College, which stood about where the Flint Institute of Arts is today. While there for two years, I had the privilege of attending Jim Baker's class in American Literature. A tall, soft-spoken, handsome man, his teaching set me on fire. From his words and recommendations came the inspiration I was looking for in my quest to write. From Jim I heard about and read and reread the works of Fitzgerald, Hemingway, Dos Passos, Steinbeck, Benét, Faulkner, Saroyan, "Red" Warren, Thomas Wolfe, and others.

One thing that I remember well about Jim's class was that when it was over each day, there was always a crowd around him, trying to talk to him and enjoying themselves. It was a real pleasure to be around him and to drink in his knowledge and way of teaching. He was always trying to catch and explain the right phrase, the hidden meaning, the implied philosophy, and his give-and-take with my classmates and me became two years of teaching at its best. Never have I enjoyed any years in a classroom as much as I did those two years under Jim Baker. I owe him—and many others would agree—a debt of gratitude for bringing great writing to the fore. I always wondered what happened to him after I graduated and went in the Army in World War II. After the war when I was back in Flint in the insurance business, I asked one day at the college. No one seemed to know where he had gone and there was no record. I would have liked to have seen him again and visited with him.

Below I am listing a few excerpts of some of the works he presented to us that had great appeal to me:

From *The Daring Young Man on the Flying Trapeze* by William Saroyan, who is much out of favor today, but his work impressed me:

'then swiftly, neatly, with the grace
of the young man on the trapeze, he was gone from his body
for an eternal moment he was all things at once;
the bird, the fish, the rodent, the reptile, and man.

An ocean of print undulated endlessly and darkly before him.
The city burned, the herded crowd rioted.
The earth circled away, and knowing that he did too,
He turned his lost face to the empty sky
And became dreamless, unalive, perfect...

From *The Human Comedy* by Saroyan:

His mother was in the yard, throwing feed to the chickens.
She watched the boy trip and fall and get up and skip again.
He came quickly and quietly and stood beside her, then went to the hen nest to look
    for eggs.
He found one. He looked at it a moment, picked it up, brought it to his mother and
    very carefully handed it to her, by which he meant what no man can guess and
    no child can remember to tell.

From *John Brown's Body* by Stephen Vincent Benét:

All day the snow fell on that Eastern town
With its soft, pelting, little, endless sigh
Of infinite flakes that brought the tall sky down
Till I could put my hands in the white sky
And taste cold scraps of Heaven on my tongue...

From *Look Homeward, Angel* by Thomas Wolfe:

A stone, a leaf, an unfound door;
of a stone, a leaf, a door.
And of all the forgotten faces.

Naked and alone we come into exile.
In her dark womb we did not know our mother's face;
From the prison of her flesh
have we come into the unspeakable
And incommunicable prison of this earth.

Which of us has known his brother?
Which of us has looked into his father's heart?
Which of us has not remained forever prison pent?
Which of us is not forever a stranger and alone?

George G. Spaulding

Charlestown, South Carolina

He is the greatest salesman I ever met. He carries in his wallet an article by Norman Vincent Peale, the renowned New York minister entitled, "The Priceless Power of Enthusiasm." Here is an excerpt:

> The president of a large company states, "If I am trying to decide between two people of fairly equal ability, I know that the one with the more enthusiasm will go further than the other because enthusiasm acts as a self-releasing power and helps focus the entire force of personality on any matter at hand. Enthusiasm is infectious; it carries all before it."

In my lifetime of 85 years, I have never known anyone who was more vital in attitude, more glad to be alive, more enthusiastic than George. We first met as freshmen at Flint Junior College in '39. *The Ann Sheridan Story* which I here repeat gives you a picture of George; in terms of attitude, the spirit of adventure, a never-say-no approach to life. It was a time I remember well as joyous, free-spirited, and an air of "let's take on all comers." It strengthened my friendship of now more than 67 years with this man.

The Ann Sheridan Story

Each year Flint Junior College held a spring dance, "The Snowball." The student body crowned a queen. If any money was made from the dance, it went for some JC project. That year (1939) if the dance made money, it would be used to purchase new basketball uniforms for Charley Trumball's squad. Peg Savage was to be the queen, and George and I were made Chairman and Co-Chairman. We were told by Charley in no uncertain terms to sell a lot of tickets. George couldn't refuse Charley—he was on the basketball squad. I couldn't refuse Charley because I was failing accounting (which I hated). Charley promised that he'd give me some extra tutelage at his house if I sold tickets.

So George and I were hooked by Charley and had to figure out how to sell a lot of tickets. The next thing that I remember we were sitting over at my house and George said to me, "I've got it. We'll write a letter to Ann Sheridan [at that time the hottest star in Hollywood] and promise her the moon if she'll come and crown the queen. That'll sell tickets quicker than anything. We'll put her up at the Durant, have the mayor give her the keys to the city and have a big parade, and present her with a brand new Buick Roadmaster."

It sounded good to me. I figured that with Ann Sheridan coming, we'd have one hell of a party.

"How are you going to write her?" I asked.

"My boss, Mr. Johnson, at the *News-Advertiser* will know," George responded. (The *Flint News-Advertiser* was Flint's second paper at that time.) "I'll get Mr. Johnson to let us put the letter we write on the front page. That'll be great publicity and I know he'll go for it." (At the time George was a part-time reporter for the paper, working in the afternoon after school.)

As for the Buick Roadmaster, the Durant Hotel, and the mayor, we didn't worry about such details. We figured the whole thing would be a gag and everyone would look at it that way. Probably we wouldn't even get an answer to our letter to Miss Sheridan.

So we wrote the letter and it did appear on the front page of Mr. Johnson's newspaper. We figured that a lot of folks had their laughs at the stunt a couple of 19 year olds were pulling. It did go over like a blast at JC and we started to sell tickets.

One day about ten days later, Bob Mogford, a friend of ours, stopped George and me in school and asked us if we'd heard yet from Ann Sheridan. We laughed and said we hadn't.

A few days later, George and I were called into the main office at school. There was a special delivery letter addressed to us and it was postmarked from Hollywood, California. We began to sweat. We took it out on the porch at JC and opened it up. Ann Sheridan was coming!

We died a little. We were in deep doo-doo. We hadn't thought about getting an answer. Now there was the matter of the mayor, the hotel, and the car. "Well," George remarked, "if you have a lemon, you might as well make lemonade."

"Let's print her reply in the *News-Advertiser*," George said. "We'll put a copy on the bulletin board here and broadcast it over the PA system. That'll sell tickets like hot cakes." After we did that, things really went into gear!

Then we went to Scott Shattuck, the manager of the Durant. After a lot of kidding, he agreed to give Ann Sheridan his best suite. We'd supply the flowers. Then we went to the mayor's office in City Hall and he was all for it. He said we could have a big parade and let the queen and Ann ride together in the first car.

But the car...the Buick Roadmaster...what to do?

Then one day my father offered to take us to meet William F. Hufstader, a Vice President of General Motors and head of Buick. He and my father had been friends for years. My dad said to George and me, "You birds are in the soup, and I'd like to see it stirred." He got us an appointment and we went up on Hamilton Avenue to Buick headquarters with my father, expecting the worst.

William F. Hufstader was a big man, standing about 6-foot-3 and weighing about 280 pounds. He sat at the end of an enormous room at a big desk and glared at us, but smiled at my father and shook hands with him. He then turned to us and gave us the business. We were called every name in the book, his words were well chosen, searing, blunt.

"You two little twerps think you're God-awful smart, giving away a Roadmaster! I've followed your little escapade and you're both lucky you aren't in jail! Who in the bloody hell do you think you are anyway?" William Hufstader's bulk loomed over us ominously.

"You two are going to work you little asses off in the dirtiest jobs I can find for you until the car is paid for. You're gonna slave and slave. And then when Miss Sheridan comes to Flint, you two birds won't even be in sight. I'll be driving Ann Sheridan if she comes, and I don't believe she's coming anyway! Before I'm through with you two, you're gonna wish you never lived! Now get the hell out of my sight and close the door when you leave!"

William F. Hufstader kicked us out of his office unceremoniously and asked my father to stay behind. We closed the door quietly. As we did, we could hear the loud guffaws inside. My dad later told me that Mr. Hufstader laughed so loudly, he brought tears to his eyes.

So what. Anyway, we were going to get the car!

Two days later, the bubble burst. George and I were walking down the hall at school when Mr. E.L. Cross, our economics teacher, called us into his office. We were at a loss to figure out what he would want of us.

"Did you two idiots take a good look at that letter from Miss Ann Sheridan?" he asked.

"Yes," we answered.

"You two have been taken by somebody. The letter is a fake."

"What do you mean?" I asked.

"The letter. It was a *personal* letter. That doesn't happen. If it had been the real McCoy, it would have come from her press agent or her movie studio. You two have been set-up by somebody."

I smelled a rat; a rat by the name of Mogford.

We located Mogford with his girlfriend, Jeanette. It all came out in a hurry. It was another of Bob Mogford's exquisite brainstorms. When he first heard of the letter George and I sent, he went to Jeanette. They composed a letter as if it came from Ann Sheridan. Then they mailed it to Jeanette's aunt who lived in Los Angeles. The aunt mailed it back to George and me by getting it postmarked in Hollywood. The rest was history.

We made a deal with Bob. He kept his part of the bargain. In return for their silence, I got him some Fox Theatre tickets in Detroit for a show Jeannette wanted to see.

Then we went ahead with our plans.

A few days before the big event, a wire came from Hollywood. Ann Sheridan, the beautiful brunette heart-throb, had become ill and her studio advised us of the news.

We paid for that telegram at Western Union. That next day, Peg Savage, our queen, received a large basket of flowers from a local florist with a card signed by Ann Sheridan.

We paid for the flowers.

Peg Savage was crowned queen.

Charley Trumbull got his new basketball uniforms.

*   *   *

I love the story about George and a Navy buddy. For many years, the Spauldings and the Brauns spent our summer vacations together, many of them at Kings Cottages that were on Lake Huron south of Oscoda. This time that I mention, we were all there and George announced to us that an old buddy from the Navy was going to be passing by in a few days and he figured out a way to welcome him with his usual style. Here's where the story gets good.

George and Kinney Brookings were young officers in the Pacific on board the U.S. Core, an aircraft escort carrier. It had approximately 800 enlisted men and officers on board. Someone found out that George had newspaper experience, so they asked him to put out a ship's newspaper. Kinney Brookings was the co-editor.

Every day one of the men would take the news off the radio and type stories, most of them heavy on sports. Then they would make duplicate copies on a mimeograph machine. To add spice to the news, Kinney came up with the idea that a sex killer should be involved.

It all started with a naked woman's body found in a trunk in New York. A detective, Cosmo Fairfax Swatch, was assigned to the case. Cosmo chased the alleged killer across the U.S. and finally apprehended him in Canada. He was identified as the "zoot-suited goon from Saskatoon." The crew of the aircraft read this story, a little of it each day, and finally the series ended.

With this in George's mind, he said to everyone, "Let's go into Oscoda to the lumber yard and get some cheap equipment and make a lot of signs. We'll spell out on the signs the story that Kinney and I made up while on the Navy ship."

So, the day that the Brookings were to hit the road north from Toledo to see the Spauldings, our little caravan equipped with signs and posters of all shapes and sizes, drove down to where the road makes a "v" at Standish (45 miles south of us) and we put our signs in for Kinney and his wife. The first one about a half-mile from Standish just read, "The zoot-suited." Up another 100 feet was the sign that merely said in bold letters, "GOON." Spread out over 45 miles were 50 signs that Kinney broke up over… A hilarious mood prevailed that day as Kinney and his wife drove into Kings Cottages…

One year when our families were together at Higgins Lake, George and I almost killed ourselves…maybe it would have been a good thing. I had a 36-pound car-top boat which I could put on the top of my station wagon. With it I had a little Johnson 2.5 horsepower motor for trolling. Next door to us was a fellow from Toledo who had a brand new 75 horsepower Martin motor. We thought it would be fun to put the 75 horsepower motor on the back of my little boat and take off. Take off we did! We flew across Higgins Lake at a gallop with the lake right up to our topsides. We could only steer it with an oar and when we got to the other side of Higgins Lake, we beached it! Then to get back…the same way. On the way back we were praying that our lives would be spared.

While George was the manager of Circle Buick in the Wall Street area of New York, he witnesses a stunt by Harold Ross and his buddies. Harold, at the time, was the editor of *The New Yorker*, and known to be a heavy drinker. He lunched at the 21 Club, where his group dreamed up practical jokes to pull. One morning two hours before lunch, they bought some street workers' uniforms, put them on over their business suits, rented a huge truck with equipment required to dig holes. A quarter block away from the "21," they barricaded off a section of the street, took their jack hammers and dug a big hole in the street. Finished with the dig, their driver took all the equipment and the truck away, and they walked into "21" for lunch, still wearing their uniforms. It was days before the big hole was filled.

Along the line of George's career in General Motors, he was made Director of Marketing for GM overseas. Later, he became the Director of Sales for Adam Opel A.G., based in Rüsselsheim, Germany. While there, he was confronted with a problem with the auto dealers in Germany, specifically one by the name of Ravenburg, the dealer in Hamburg. He had been an "ace" on the German Luftwaffe on the eastern front during World War II. Ravenburg tried to oust George from his position. George came up with a plan which finally made peace and satisfied the auto dealers. Three years later, George was promoted to Sales Manager of Pontiac Motor, and these same German dealers threw George and Dorie, his wife, a farewell party in the famous Kronberg Castle. During the evening's festivities, Ravenburg took back all the bad remarks he had made about George. While George was with Opel, it became the Number 1 passenger car in Germany, displacing Volkswagen.

One of George's greatest achievements in his lifetime of sales and service was his time, and is his time at the College of Charlestown, South Carolina. A labor of love, without any remuneration, he started a course called "Real World 101." It was a three hour per week course, and became very popular with the students. It concerned itself with the world economy, the gross national product, credit, and investment banking, a course which helped students prepare for the job market. Known at that time as an "Executive in Residence," his resume reads like a "Who's Who in Business."

- Managed some of the largest auto dealers in the United States (Applegate Chevrolet in Flint, Michigan; 3 Buick retail stores; and founded Circle Buick in New York City.

- Worked 25 years with four General Motors divisions. Buick (Retail Sales); established Opel import programs. Chevrolet (Assistant Regional Manager in Washington, D.C. and Director of Chevrolet National Service Operations in Detroit); Vice President of GM Overseas Operations); General Sales Manager at Pontiac.

- President of the Michigan Auto Dealers Association.

- President of Big Brothers in Flint, Michigan.

- Chairman of the Board of Governors, College of Charleston in South Carolina.

Some years ago I wrote this about George: "It is time to introduce you to one of the most imaginative and droll personalities I've ever had the pleasure of knowing. A person who always managed to be where the action was, one who could take a lemon and make lemonade out of it, one who through all the years possessed a brand of humor hard to beat. Friends after all these years; our paths cross once in a while when he comes to visit his son and family in the Flint area."

*   *   *

One day I stood at the bottom steps at JC with George. We were eyeing the girls on the porch. It was a Friday afternoon and the girls were sitting on the porch waiting for a date. "Who's that good-looking brunette?" I asked George. He knew all the gals. "I'll introduce you," he said. He did, and I married her.

Robert J. Mogford

Flint, Michigan

Before I took off in a Liberty ship for Europe during World War II, I had a telephone call from my parents. They told me that Bob had been killed coming back from a raid on Germany. He was piloting a B-24, and in an emergency landing, the plane blew-up. It's over 60 years later and I still think about the antics of Robert J. Mogford at Flint Junior College in the years '39 and '40. What he organized with a bunch of his friends including yours truly still gives me a chuckle.

One day he got a number of us in the Men's Club room in the basement of JC, a dingy, poorly-lighted room, and he proceeded to pass out a whole bunch of magazines and a set of cheap scissors to everyone. Then he showed us one ad that he wanted clipped out. The ad was similar to many in those days in magazines like *Popular Science*, *Field and Stream*, *Good Housekeeping*, *Colliers*, *Liberty*, etc. We had dozens and dozens of magazines to look at. For a few dimes, you could fill out this ad and get a sample of something in the mail. The samples were hair tonic, razor blades, unmentionable ladies products, aspirin, Tums, etc. We found the ads, cut them out, and signed Dean Shattuck's name and his address at JC. In about two weeks, the dean's office was besieged by every product known to man.

Another time he assembled us again. He had Flint divided into sections. Two-man teams were to work together the following Saturday night and to take what Bob presented us with: skeleton keys. Our job was to put these keys at night in every saloon and restaurant and outhouse in Flint where someone would find them and call Dean Shattuck. My beat that Saturday night with Keith Norwalk was Saginaw Street from Fisher Body on Hemphill Road in the south to Carpenter Road in the north end. Keith and I put those keys in every bar and gas station all along the route. I understood, from a friend in his office, that the dean was pestered for two weeks with calls from those who found the keys.

To cap these antics, Bob saw me at JC one Friday afternoon and announced that he had a pail of whitewash. If we could get a long ladder, we could get up on the roof of the powerhouse facing JC and put some letters on it that spelled "BEWARE FROSH." I was game. We got my dad's long ladder and on a Saturday night very late, we took the ladder and traipsed through Woodlawn Park, across East Court Street, behind Whittier Junior High, past Central High, until we stood on the back side of the powerhouse. We climbed the ladder on a moonless night and did our deed. Halfway through, a police car came along, and shone its lights. Luckily, they didn't beam upwards toward us.

One day Bob said to me back in '39, "We're going to get in this war against Germany. I know it." So he enrolled in a flying course at Bishop Airport. One day during school, his bride-to-be, Jeanette Rumbold, had a call from him from the airport. He told her to be on the porch at JC at noon and that he would fly over and waggle his wings. The word got around and we were waiting for him that noon. Soon a little green Piper Cub came over the main building at Flint Central with Bob flying low. When he passed JC, he waggled his wings and waved, then threw a kiss at Jeanette. Dean Shattuck looked out his window and then called Bishop Airport and had Bob grounded.

I few years ago, I started a scholarship at Mott College (the successor to the old Flint JC) in Bob's honor. Each year a student receives it. I think of him many times and how he gave his life for his country.

Addison Baines Carwile

Abbeville, South Carolina

His good friends called him *ABC*. The first time I met him, he was a major at Laughlin Air Force base near Del Rio, Texas in the winter of 1943. I had just washed out of the Air Corps with some eye deficiency and had been sent to Del Rio. While there, I was sitting in a corridor with other enlisted men and we were lower than a snake underground because of having washed out. A burly, red-faced captain strode out of a room, looked at us, and asked, "Any of you men ever had any ration board experience?" I said hurriedly, "Yes, sir." He said, "Come in my office." I went in, saluted him, and he said, "Tell me about it, young man." The only experience I had had was back in '42 while waiting to be called into the service. I had volunteered one day to help pass out ration stamps at some office. But, I told the captain (because I was tired of sitting on my duff and doing nothing), "Sir, I was the No. 2 man in Genesee County on the ration board for a year." That was all the captain wanted to know. He said, "Okay, you are a corporal as of right now. Get your stripes from your sergeant at your barracks and report to me tomorrow" at such-and-such a place.

For the next month and a half, all I did was supervise the work of two civilian women. We gave ration stamps to almost 4,700 soldiers, aviators, and civilians working on the base. It was boring work, and because of it and the hours, I never had any basic training. In the meantime, I called Sally and she told me she wanted to get married. I had promised her if I ended up doing clerical work in the Army with no chance for action we'd get married. So I applied for a three day leave plus travel, went home, and we were married June 4th at the little chapel in the First Presbyterian Church. Then, after one night at Ft. Shelby in Detroit, we took a troop train to Del Rio. I remember that one night on the train I had to sleep on a pile of dirty towels between two train cars, while Sally sat up next to some soldier who wouldn't let me sit down.

When we got to Del Rio, there was a sign on the bulletin board saying that you could apply for officer candidate school (OCS). I figured that I had as good a chance as anyone and I didn't want to spend the war rationing tires and gas. So I applied. A major and two captains interviewed me, the major being Addison Carwile. The first question he casually asked me was,

"You've had your basic training, haven't you, Corporal?" I said, "Yes," not realizing that some day in the near future I was in for a peck of trouble. A month went by. Sally and I had rented a room with a bath in old Del Rio, where we ran into some friends—one of them Gordon Anderson from Minnesota, who is still a close friend today. There was a large spring in Del Rio where everyone seemed to congregate. I also noticed that many of the buildings and some of the streets were named for a person who I later found out was the infamous Dr. Brinkley, who advertised goat glands to make men sexually proficient. (He was later kicked out of the state and set up a powerful radio broadcast station across the river in Via Cuna, Mexico.)

Then one day Gordon Anderson said to me, "You're going to OCS. It's on the bulletin board." I reported to an office and Major Carwile was there. He congratulated me and said my orders were being typed. He said I'd leave in about a week. Then he said to me, "My wife lives on our farm just out of Abbeville, South Carolina. I'm having the order drawn in such a way that, on your way to Camp Davis in North Carolina [which is just outside of Wilmington] you'll have a day and night to spend with her. Her name is Alice Rhen. When you get to camp, pick up the phone and call me collect. Here's the number. Put it in your billfold. Tell me how she's getting along."

With that, I saluted again. When I got in to Del Rio that night to be with Sally, we had just one week together before I took off for OCS. She headed back to Flint and I hopped a train east. I had forgotten about my comment regarding basic training.

I made a brief stopover at Abbeville, a sleepy southern town where Jefferson Davis spent his last few moments with his cabinet before being apprehended on the road south. I visited Alice with her home cooking and southern hospitality, and then moved on to a depot near Wilmington. As I disembarked, a captain thrust a rifle in my hands and ordered me to give close-order drill to all the men getting off the train. This was one of the toughest times in my young life because I'd never had to stand drill or retreat and didn't even know how to give orders or handle a rifle. It was then that the captain barked at me, "You're going back to Del Rio or I'll make a man out of you in two weeks of boot camp." Ninety days and two weeks later, I had my gold bars pinned on by the same captain. He made me face the company as he said with some trace of sarcasm and irritation, "I want to introduce you to 2nd Lt. Philip J. Braun 010621132. He is the most improved man in this company, and I'll tell you why: he had more room for improvement than any man I've ever known."

The next time I met Addison Carwile was back at his home in Abbeville after the war on the farm where Alice called him *Squire*. He still stood ram-rod straight and was a soil conservationist and state senator, representing South Carolina from his district. He had been discharged from the Army as a full Colonel serving on MacArthur's staff in the Philippines and having been in many of the island-hopping episodes in the southwest Pacific before the surrender of Japan.

One other time when Sally and I visited Alice and the Squire on the way to Florida, he told me proudly that as a dirt farmer he was still able to put four children through college. He said they could go wherever they wanted to, as long as it was Clemson, his alma mater.

The last time I saw the Squire was several years ago when we were in Columbia, South Carolina and the Senate was in session. The Squire introduced us to a filled audience as "Yankee friends" and then proudly took us to the west façade of the building so he could show us the scars of battle where Sherman's artillery balls bounced off the walls. He also told me that if I look at any southern square in any little southern town, the battlefield monument to the Civil War days always faces south. Addison Baines Carwile was a true southern gentleman.

Lennetta B. Coney

Flint, Michigan

A few years ago, Bob Robison invited me to lunch at the Flint Golf Club. I met Lennetta Coney. I was very impressed by her gracious manner and poise. As a grad of the old Junior College in 1940, and having presented the Phil J. Braun Cup—given by my father at the time that I entered the Air Corps in Word War II—I was somewhat aware of Mott College and its drive to develop the potential of its students. But I was not aware of the interesting, huge role that Lennetta played. The conversation around the table that day intrigued me. It drew me further into the efforts of this outstanding African-American woman, whose mother-in-law (Cloteal Coney), had been in my class in high school at the old Flint Northern.

Lennetta is an amazing, absorbing, wholesome woman whose work effort has produced some outstanding results at Mott. She holds the title of President of the Foundation for Mott Community College (MCC) and Director of Mott Institutional Development.

As I started to become more involved at Mott (because of my respect and admiration for Lennetta), it was my pleasure, and that of some of my associates of the Northern High Alumni Association, to invite her to the Viking room at Northern. From this meeting and future discussions came the birth and success of the Mott Alumni Association, as well as the room in which proud alumni are featured and scholarships given.

Lennetta has worked as a Mott Community College administrator for 15 years. In her two capacities noted above, she has been directly responsible for private fund-raising, special events, and multi-cultural affairs at MCC. A few weeks ago (written as of April 2005), Fran Gumpper and I had the pleasure of attending an excellent talk given by the film maker and outspoken personage of Spike Lee to an audience of nearly 1,500 people. This was part of the Ballenger Series, all very well coordinated and achieved under Lennetta's direction.

As the Chief Development Officer of the Foundation, Lennetta has seen the foundation grow fiscally from some $194,000 to its current status of $3 million. In addition, she holds the position of Director for Region V (Indiana, Illinois, Minnesota, Wisconsin, Ohio, and Ontario) for the Council of Resource Development, the national organization for community college fund-raising.

Prior to coming to Mott, Lennetta served as a Senior Account Executive for a major advertising agency, working on accounts such as Wendy's, Equitable Life Insurance, and others. At one time she was a buyer for Garfinkels. Lennetta possesses a bachelor's degree from Howard University, a master's in advertising from Michigan State, and has done post-graduate doctoral work also at State.

Lennetta has been the recipient of the Woman of the Year award from the National Association of Women in Higher Education, the Choice Award from the Flint Club of Negro Business and Professional Women, a Community Service award from the Eta Phi Beta Sorority, Inc., and the Martin Luther King Jr. award. She was a recent nominee for both the YWCA's Women of Achievement and the Chamber of Commerce's Athena awards.

A dynamo of a woman, Lennetta Coney has greatly strengthened Mott College in its drive to better educate young people, and is much loved by all she meets. It has been a great pleasure to know her and be a friend.

Jim Mitchell

Flint, Michigan

I had a call at the office one day many years ago. It happened to be the same day that the Shrine Circus was folding its tents and preparing to depart from Flint after a successful show at the IMA.

The caller on the phone was Jim Mitchell, the manager of the boys department at JC Penney. He wanted to know whether I was going to attend Junior Chamber that night in the Home Dairy building on Kearsley Street. I said that I planned on it, and he said, "How would you like to take Sheriff Tom Wolcott's mule into the meeting?" I thought that might be fun and asked how we might accomplish that little feat. Knowing Jim, who was a practical joker par excellence, I was ready for his answer. He said, "I'm borrowing the mule tonight. He's out at the stables on Miller Road. We can pick up the mule with a truck I have and get him down to the old PM depot behind Jimmy Rice's cab stand. Then we can lead in to the alley behind the Home Dairy. I'll pick you up at your house at 5:30, get a quick supper, and tell Sally you're going to a special meeting of Junior Chamber."

I said, "Okay." I had been on some projects with Jim before and they were something. He had a devious mind. You could expect anything. Jim picked me up and we went out to the stables. We found "Bessie" and with some effort, we loaded her into the truck. We went downtown to the old PM loading dock on South Grand Traverse Street. When we got her off the back of the truck onto a ramp, we found that we had a problem. Bessie would only turn left. That required a lesson in geography trying to figure out how to get her into Buckham Alley behind the Home Dairy.

By this time it was snowing to beat the band as we headed north on South Saginaw Street at dusk and began to pass C.S. Mott's Smith-Bridgman Department Store. Coming down the street toward us in a long file were the elephants from the circus as they were being led south to the 14th Street railroad depot. As we passed them, Bessie farted and the elephants returned the favor. Then the circus attendants went into show business by cleaning up after them. I thought that Bessie was just recognizing the circus. It seemed like professional courtesy.

Ahead of us lay Kearsley Street and the Home Dairy. This was not what Bessie wanted at all with her left turn attitude. We had to go west on Kearsley instead of east and try to figure it out from there. By this time, our vision was cut down to a few feet by the heavy snow. A few of the cars passing us honked their horns in recognition of the mule. That was a nice touch.

Finally, and by this time it was dark, we arrived at the back of the Home Dairy and got Bessie inside a service elevator. This was not what she wanted. She proceeded to kick the sides of the elevator and raise hell. At this juncture, Jim decided that we had best retreat.

I give Bessie credit. Once out in the alley, her ways were peaceful. We found our way back to the truck. Junior Chamber missed a good show. Bessie saw the elephants. We didn't end up in jail.

Justice Robert Jackson

Jamestown, New York

"Sparky" and Justice Jackson, or "How I Bought an Insurance Agency..."

The day World War II ended I was with my platoon in the northern suburbs of Munich, Germany. We were guarding a railroad center containing many boxcars still loaded with munitions for the beaten Wehrmacht. My outfit, with my platoon sergeant Frank Piedigrossi, had landed at Oran in North Africa during the winter of '42. They had faced fierce fighting from the French during the landing, losing three men in the platoon I was later to join in France. Because of their extended time in Europe, my outfit knew they would be going back to the states soon, and I would be left high and dry, since I hadn't entered Italy until June 24, 1944. Until late July, we were stationed near Munich in the little village of Prien. We spent most of our time there sitting on our duffs, other than the time we took boats to a nearby island in the lake and found a warehouse replete with cognac and long cigars specially made for Goering. I had a box of those cigars in my jeep for a month.

One day my outfit got orders to move out to the coast and go home. I talked to my colonel and he advised me to take Jimmy Gold, my wonderful jeep driver and friend, and go down the Autobahn to Salzburg where a full-bird colonel was in charge of redeployment of troops. Some of the troops were heading for the Far East and the war still on with Japan.

With trepidation (because I didn't want to end up in the Far East), Jimmy and I drove to Salzberg. I reported in to the bird colonel. About the time I saluted him, the first question out of the box was, "Lieutenant, have you ever had any hotel experience?" Sometimes a little lie doesn't hurt anybody. Sometimes, a big lie is called for. It was time for the big lie. "Yes, sir," I said with a straight face, feeling no guilt. "I ran the Braun Hotel in Petoskey, Michigan for three years before the war. It had been my father's brother's hotel, and I ran it to help the widow after her husband died." I waited, thinking there would be more questions, that I would have to confess that the hotel had 13 rooms, 2 baths, and a small lunch counter on the first floor. No questions came. The colonel said, "I have an opening for two officers of 1st Lieutenant or above to run the

Berchtesgaden Hof, the central hotel in Berchtesgaden, only six kilometers from the Berghof and Eagles Nest of Hitler. He said the opening was the following month, that he would have my orders cut before I left to go back to Prien. I thanked the colonel and saluted him. Jimmy and I went back to Prien. Shortly afterwards, I was in Berchtesgaden and in the hotel, meeting Harry Barnes, a captain, who was to run the hotel with me.

I was at the hotel then in the summer of '45 until I left for the States sometime the following March. Our duties were minimal because we had an efficient staff with a maitre'd, Herr Geyer, who was excellent. Harry and I had a suite with a bell cord which we'd ring early in the morning. Sometimes Geyer would appear with a plate of fresh eggs and ham, fresh strawberries, and we'd split a bottle of champagne. A tough life for a 23 year old like myself.

One week I ran the hotel (with Geyer doing most of the work), which consisted of getting rations, overseeing the help, the cleaning, the dining room, the kitchen, the bar, and entertainment in the cellar. That week Harry's job was to take our guests (majors and above of all the Allied Forces) to the Berghof (what was left of it) and the Eagles Nest and on trips with sleds and horses into the mountains. We figured out a way to have ice skating on a large patio in the back of the hotel facing the Watzmann Mountain range. During that week around the Christmas holidays, while I happened to be on the check-in desk, a group came in. It was Justice Jackson, his son, and a number of the young attorneys who were preparing the briefs for the upcoming trial of the high ranking Nazis in Nuremberg. After checking everyone into their rooms, I had a call from Justice Jackson. He wondered if a trip could be arranged around the area and up into the mountains for him and his son. I talked to Harry and he found a sled and two sturdy horses. We arranged a picnic lunch for the justice and his son for the next day. When they arrived back later the next day, I asked the justice if I could take a picture of the two of them in the sled. They agreed. After I had taken the picture, I had the film taken to a lab I knew of in the village. I had the lab develop and enlarge the picture, and put into a frame for the justice and his son. I then presented it to them before they left for Nuremberg.

Now we switch gears—I take you to the Eisenhower years in the White House, the late 50s. Ike and his administration had succeeded (through Congress) in starting a network of super-highways all across the country. With this came what was known in those days as the Eisenhower Highway Safety Congress, a meeting held each year in Washington attended by many interested corporations. The insurance industry played a part in those meetings and it was decided that two representatives of the insurance industry from each state should come to the conference. Lo and behold, the two from Michigan were both from Flint, who turned out to be my old friend and competitor, "Sparky" Hale and myself. I don't know the reasoning for the picking. Sparky and I stepped on the train at the 12th Street station and went to Washington. At the time I was trying to buy Sparky's agency because he was in his 60s and ready to retire. I knew that Sparky liked Wild Turkey bourbon so I put some in my luggage. On the way to Washington, we had a few belts and a great time. Sparky and his lovely wife Bess and I had been friends for years.

The conference lasted three days. Representatives from many industries took part: trucking, insurance, medical, etc. At the end of the conference, we had a whole afternoon before we were to step on the train. I said to Sparky, "There's a place I want you and me to see." I took him in a cab to the Supreme Court building. I thought Justice Jackson might be in, and while he wouldn't remember me from a sack of potatoes, it would be worth the trip and would surprise Sparky.

I didn't know whether the court was in session and if there was even a chance to say "Hello" to the justice. In those days, you went around to a side entrance and gave your calling card to a manservant. I wrote on my business card that I had been at the Berchtesgaden Hof when he was there. The servant came back and said, "The justice can see you for five minutes." We went into his quarters and there, above his desk, flew four flags made out of paratroop silk: one American, one British, one French and one Russian. They had hung over the docket during the Nuremberg trials. Then, to my surprise, on his desk stood the framed picture I had taken of the justice and his son back in '45. I mentioned that to the justice and he smiled. He said he had had a great time at the Hof with his son.

On the way back to Flint on the train later that day, Sparky talked about meeting Justice Jackson and then we got down to business. By the time we got to Flint, I bought his agency.

Thomas Shapton Purdy

Flint, Michigan

Student at old Flint Northern, track man, graduate with honors at Michigan Tech at Houghton, father, fighter pilot in World War II, war hero, fisherman…I should add environmentalist… A little man in height, but a Bantam-rooster in action, one of my close friends. Our parents both had cottages at what was then called Long Lake (later named Lake Fenton), just one mile north of Fenton, Michigan.

Here at the lake, Tom and I fished for bullheads late at night, built a tree shanty up 20 feet in the air behind the Purdy cottage, with a tin runner to the ground for our urine. It was a place that only the two of us could occupy unless with our permission. Tom was a terrific fist-fighter who many times bloodied his older brother in their contests of will.

When we were a little older and were at the lake in the summer, Tom drove a Model T and I stood on the running board and threw folded newspapers onto our customers' lawns, sometimes landing them in prize flowerbeds to the ire of the women. We had the Detroit Free Press, the Detroit Times, the Detroit News, and the Flint Journal (commonly known as the Flint Urinal). We peddled both sides of Orrs Point and down toward Fenton to the south end of the lake. One customer, Hector Rabazzani, a senior engineer at Buick, took all four papers from us.

One of Tom's close friends in high school was Bud Thatcher. Bud played in the band and thrilled audiences with his triple-tonguing cornet on the "Flight of the Bumblebee." As close as the two of them were, usually they ended up fist-fighting about once a month and then when they were tired, shook hands.

Tom carried a little music box that his mother gave him that had been attached to a flower arrangement. One day he took it to Northern High School. I was in a couple of his classes, and was there in Les Ehrbright's class that day when he put the music box (which played "How Dry I Am") under the yellow radiator near the pencil sharpener. It drove Ehrbright crazy.

Tom had a great friend in one of the teachers, Stan Kuick, who was on Houston's football staff as line coach. One summer, Stan took Tom up into northern Canada and they lived off the land while they hunted and fished.

In the war years, Tom started flying P-38 Lightnings over Africa and finally was moved with his squadron to Bari, Italy, where he flew Lightnings as far north as Munich, over the Alps, in protection of our bombers. He also flew cover on a couple of missions over Ploesti, Romania, where the great oil fields were. He was awarded the Silver Star and never wanted to show it to anybody.

Fishing was Tom's greatest love. He and his brother (with whom he still fought) had a cabin in the woods along the south branch of the AuSable east of Grayling. Here, Tom began night fishing for the big browns. The AuSable has some mighty browns, some of them going close to 30-inches, and they feed at night. When you stand still in the middle of a warm night during fish-fly hatch (mid-June) and shine a flashlight directly above you, there are thousands of fish-flies. If you don't keep your mouth closed, you're eating them! One night about 11:00 Tom was out listening to the browns feeding (which I can only say sounds like "glop"). He had a bait which was unlawful, although that didn't mean anything to Tom. The bait was called the Deadly Streamer and it had treble hooks. When it was thrown, it hit the water with a splash. Suddenly Tom heard a big brown feeding and threw in the Deadly Streamer. The fish took it and pulled Purdy into the stream. He was completely wet...but happy. He said he fought the fish for a half an hour, almost drowning in the effort, but finally landed it. Tom carried a jacklight attached to his hat. The fish measured a little over 27-inches and was a monster. He took it back to his cabin along the river and could hardly wait until 8:00 in the morning when the first store at Ma Deeters at Luzerne opened. He entered the fish in the annual contest and lost the contest by one-half inch. I fished many times with Tom, but never fared well after dusk. To me the dark never had any appeal.

In the 50s (when Tom lived at the lake year round with his wife and two daughters) Long Lake was getting polluted. Some owners had their sewage draining into the lake. Tom put on a one-man campaign, going door-to-door, urging owners to clean up their act. He did it for over three years and enlisted some help from the state. Finally, with his efforts and efforts of others who later joined him, the lake was cleaned up. It was cleaned up to the point that walleye pike fingerlings were introduced in the 60s or 70s. Today, people are catching good-sized clean walleyes out of Lake Fenton.

I took Purdy and a bunch of my friends on a western fishing trip to the ABarA on the North Platte in Wyoming. Purdy had a ball. Another time in the 60s, just after Mother's Day, we headed to Canada. Sixty-some miles north of the Sault, we took a trailhead to a small lake that still had ice around its edges. We had axes, hammers, some boards and nails that we used to build two rafts, each big enough to hold two men. We fished that day with Hendrickson flies. The squaretails were hot for that fly. We caught 18-inch native brook trout and cooked them on shore for dinner. It was perhaps the best trip we ever made.

Purdy had a massive heart attack when he was in his 60s and I helped bury him. I cried like a baby.

John Woollam, Ph.D.

Lincoln, Nebraska

One of the most interesting experiences in my life was spent with John Woollam about ten years ago. Sally and I had agreed when we were living in Florida that it would be alright for me to photograph sand hill cranes along the Platte River in Nebraska. Each March since millions of years ago, the sand hill cranes and other birds have followed a migratory path from deep in the south along the Gulf of Mexico to the Arctic. One of their stopping points has been the Platte in a section perhaps 50 miles long, west of Lincoln. At the time, John was a full professor of physics at the University of Nebraska and had invited me to join him in photographing the birds.

After Sally and I arrived in Lincoln, John and I drove further west for three days. The blinds we were in were not located close enough to the Platte River. But late one afternoon, after we had left a blind and taken a few photographs, we stood on a bridge near Kearney, Nebraska. As dusk settled, you could begin to hear the sounds of the cranes leaving the cornfields. They were headed for the river where they would spend the night. We stood on the bridge with an old farmer who said he'd witnessed this sight for a couple of weeks at this time of dusk. Suddenly the noise became louder and louder and the birds began to appear over head. John and I probably witnessed at least 10,000 birds coming back into the river for the night. It was as if we were watching what I can only call *creation*. It was, with the sound of the cranes (which is like a broken washing-machine sound), one of the most exciting and fascinating nights I had ever spent in my life and I will never forget the thrill.

John Woollam. How can I do him justice in describing the man and his personality? Professor, inventor, NASA worker, husband, father, industrialist, scientist, philanthropist, etc. When I heard that he had been given an honorary doctorate by the Linkoping University in Linkoping, Sweden in 2004, I was very, very pleased. He was chosen because of decades of published research in materials science, including ellipsometry; more than a decade of collaboration with Swedish researchers; and because of the prominence of John's own company. The ellipsometry instruments his company produces are especially prominent among the world's researchers.

At first when I knew John I didn't know what ellipsometry was all about. I asked him. When he was through, I still didn't. In 1987 he started a company in Nebraska that makes this machine. It is an optic instrument that uses polarized light for research and development on thin films and surfaces. His customers are in numerous industries such as automotive, glass and coatings on glass, companies that manufacture coatings for such things as decorative coatings on watch bands and bumpers, read-write heads in computers, integrated circuits for computers, coatings for razor blades and flat panel displays (e.g. laptop computers and flat panel TVs). As a professor of physics, John began to hire his graduate students and today his firm has some 35 employees, most of them grads of his. For many years he also headed the Cryophysics Section as a Research Scientist at the NASA Lewis Research Center.

John has built a solid reputation as a scientist, known world-wide, yet is very quiet-spoken and almost shy.

I admire him for another reason of a very personal nature. John has two very lovely daughters and a fine wife, Cindy. His first wife, Mary Lynn, was the daughter of one of my closest friends. She was a music major at Oberlin in Ohio. Early in their marriage after the birth of the two girls, Mary Lynn was diagnosed with MS. She became hospitalized for over 30 years and was visited regularly by John and the girls as they grew into womanhood. John was very loving and good to Mary Lynn. I was proud of the way he handled himself and the great tragedy that had befallen his family.

As a boy, John fell in love with sailing. He has sailed for many years, keeping a large sailboat at St. Joseph, Michigan. He and Cindy (and Mary Lynn in the early years of their marriage) sailed regularly and for great distances on the Great Lakes and in the Caribbean.

In addition to that wonderful hobby, John is a well-known conservationist and has contributed handsomely to many outstanding conservation projects in the Midwest. He is in the process of purchasing a nature preserve on Beaver Island off Charlevoix, Michigan. In addition, John supports many scholarships at Kenyon College, Teachers College, and the College of Engineering at the University of Nebraska.

In every endeavor in which he continues to be involved, he amazes me with his energy.

Mordecai Finklestein

New York, New York

If Mordecai wasn't the Class Valedictorian in my class at Flint Northern is '38, he must have been very close to the top. He and my great friend, Bill Billings, kept winning the city table tennis honors in those days. I remember during the union sit-down strike of '36-'37, how four of us in my old car drove down Chevrolet Avenue after school one day. The strikers waved to us from the roof top of a building. It was then that we decided we should drive downtown and look for girls. That was then the past-time, and still is. Mordecai, Bill, and Girardin O'Sullivan (Sully) were in the car with me, and as we passed a motorized policeman on Saginaw Street, Mordecai thumbed his nose at the cop. The policeman chased us and stopped us at the corner of Saginaw and Second (Walgreen's in those days).

I showed the policeman my drivers license and he asked each of us what our names were. Mordecai, sitting in the back, said, "Mordecai Finklestein." The policeman answered, "Don't be funny, son, what's your name?" Mordecai repeated it and the policeman said, "Damn, boy. You got a problem, haven't you?" Then the policeman let us go with a warning, and we sat back in the car and roared.

Mordecai entered the University of Michigan in Ann Arbor. What happened is only hearsay. He did flunk out because he spent most of his time gambling. Then his father, who was a top engineer at Buick, is to have said to him, "You're going to work here at Buick until you've paid for your education at Michigan. You'll re-enter. You'll graduate with honors or the family will disown you." Makes a good story, anyway. As the story goes, Mordecai worked at Buick, got back in Michigan, graduated with honors as an attorney, and went on to become president of the Amalgamated Garment Workers Union of New York city. By then he had changed his name to Murray Finley, had put on about 150 pounds, and returned for our 50th high school reunion with his wife. He charmed everyone.

Richard Pohrt

Ann Arbor, Michigan

As an older teenager, I had an old car to bang around in. One of my favorite haunts up in northern Michigan was that stretch between Harbor Springs and Cross Village, a beautiful tree-lined canopy of maple and birch over the road that burned with color in the fall and said to me, "This is Indian country." It was Indian country and in it lived Dick Pohrt with his unbelievable, first-rate collection of Plains Indian raiment and goods, collected year-by-year by him and his associate in their trips west, where they lived with the Indians in Montana. I would sit and listen to Dick as he told me of his adventures with the Gros Ventre Indians.

When Dick had been a teenager at Whittier Junior High in Flint, he had been fascinated by reading of the Indians of the West. With the approval of his family (which must have been something to think about), he headed west in his car and had lived on the Indian reservations—no mean accomplishment. It was here that he started his collection which grew and grew. One year when I was fishing the rivers north of Yellowstone Park, I met a great friend of his who made a living tanning deer hides and selling them to the Indians. He lived in a small settlement near Big Timber, Montana. He spent one afternoon regaling me with tales of Dick Pohrt.

Much of that wonderful collection is now the property of the Detroit Institute of Arts. A few of us, including Sue Hamady, recognized the value and importance of the collection and wanted it for the Flint Institute of Arts. We only succeeded in a minor way, much to our chagrin.

I thought so much of Dick and his ability that I recommended him to the Central High School Alumni Association and they presented him with the Distinguished Fellow designation one year. Some years later, we at Flint Northern recognized his youngest son, Tom, for the beautiful sensitivity in his drawings. Many of them illustrated Indian legends that are treasured and highly regarded by collectors.

When you read the obituary of Dick Pohrt, you realize how this man was held in such high regard by some of the great institutions of this country. For example, the Cranbrook Institute of Science; the Buffalo Bill Historical Museum in Cody, Wyoming; the Sloan Museum in Flint;

and the Board of American Indian Art Museum. Dick passed his heritage on to his three sons, all accomplished men in their own right.

Dick Pohrt was an original.

Edmund Love

Flushing, Michigan

Student at Flint Northern, teacher at Flint Northern, track coach, military historian, novelist, speech writer, one of the founders of the Northern High School Alumni Association, honored by Northern as a Distinguished Alumni, keynote speaker at Northern for the dedication of the new school in 1973 . . .

Harper's Magazine occasionally publishes a list of books to read, and when they do, *The Situation in Flushing* by Ed Love is always on the list. In addition to that, he wrote *Subways are for Sleeping, Hanging On* (a book about the depression days in Flint), and others. While at the University of Michigan he vied for the Hopwood Award, the annual literary award, and was in second place to Arthur Miller of *Death of a Salesman* fame.

I had the great pleasure after World War II of knowing both Ed and his lovely wife, Ann, who lived poor as church mice in a three room apartment across from Flint Central.

On one occasion, he was a speaker at our Northern Honors night and told about the old days at Northern on Magellan Street where the only way kids could run track in 1928-29 was to wait until school was over and then run on the third floor of the building. He also told about a track meet later with Flint Central in which one of the Northern kids was winning, but as he rounded the final turn his pants fell down. (The pants and suits of the track men were made by the boys' mothers.)

Some years back I took a fascinating course in writing from Ed at Mott College. I learned a lot, he being very engaging, witty, and an excellent speaker and teacher. During the course, one of the students asked, "What do you do when you have writer's block?" His answer, if you could believe Ed—he had a reputation for sometimes stretching a good story—was this:

Writer's block—yes . . . I once had a professor of literature at the U of M who had some books to his credit. The question was asked of him and he answered this way: "When I had this problem, I went to the kitchen and got out five cereal bowls. Then I got some lined paper and on one paper I wrote all the names I could think of that were men, like Perry, Tom, Bill, etc. Then I took all of those names and put them in the bowl. In the next bowl I put all the names of women; the next bowl, the names of cities; the next bowl, the names of states; and final bowl, the names of pets, like dogs and cats, etc.

Then I took one name out of each bowl and perhaps I ended up with Mary and Bill and Newark, Georgia and Fido. Then I got out my atlas and looked to see if I could find a Newark, Georgia. I did, and I got into my car, drove there and sat in a cheap hotel for days until I had finished a short story using the five names. I sent it in to *Reader's Digest* and other sources. It was accepted and I got a check for $400. Believe it if you will.

Another night in class, Ed told how he was made to look silly and lost the chance for a good story. At the time, he was a major and a military historian on the island of Espirito Santo in the South Pacific. His boss, a general, called him one day and told him that a Lt. Commander from the Navy was visiting the island and Ed had to entertain him for four days. He was to take him around the island, which had for some time been in Jap hands. Ed met Lt. Commander James Michener (whose name at the time didn't mean anything special to Ed). Ed introduced Michener to a Frenchman who was an ocean watcher for the U.S. forces and working against the Japs. He also took him around and introduced him to some Navy waves and others. Out of this visit by Michener came *Tales of the South Pacific* starring Mary Martin and Enzio Pinza (Pinza playing the part of the French man who was the ocean watcher)...

I admired Ed and used to read his column in the *Flint Journal*. One that I particularly remember was the story of the Hollywood Grill with Bob and Fanny Newblatt. The Hollywood Grill was just north of downtown across from the Durant Hotel on N. Saginaw Street where Bob cooked and Fanny insulted the patrons . . .

Frank Piedigrossi

Cortland, New York

On June 1, 1944 my Liberty Ship left in a huge convoy from Hampton Roads, Virginia; its destination unknown to me. It was five days before the Normandy invasion. My old outfit at Camp Stewart, an anti-aircraft group consisting of 20 mm. Bofors and half-tracks equipped with machine guns, was broken up in April of that year. The War Department figured with strong allied air power, it could use most of the anti-aircraft men in the infantry, what with the reduced effectiveness of the Nazi air machine.

I became a replacement officer headed for the infantry. Upon landing in Naples, Italy on June 24, I was assigned to the Seventh Army in the 3rd Division as a junior heavy-weapons specialist (infantry). I trained troops at what was then called the Valley of the Purple Heart north of Casserta, Italy.

On August 16, my outfit landed on D-plus 2 near St. Tropez, France and moved rapidly inland. I was one of the lucky ones, landing one day after the invasion forces, and my outfit took few casualties. We had the krauts on the run.

After a few days, we were put into box cars (40 and 8's) that still smelled of horse dung, and we moved north to Grenoble, France. Again, here I trained troops. By the middle of September I again was put in a 40 and 8 and headed north. Somewhere on that trip north, I came down with a serious attack of asthma. I was taken off the train at Epinal, France and put in a French hospital. I was there two weeks in which time a decision was made. I could either be discharged from the Army and sent back to the states (which was mortifying to me), or I could be reassigned to a Bofors anti-aircraft outfit, the 436th, at Luneville. I jumped at the chance to do the latter.

Sometime early in October I ended up at the 436th headquarters. I was assigned as an assistant platoon leader under Marve Fisher, a 1st looey, and here met my platoon sergeant, a grizzled veteran of the invasion of North Africa at Oran, where the 436th lost some men to French forces defending the city. It was one of the real breaks for me in the war. Frank

Piedigrossi was my platoon sergeant from then until the end of the war on May 8, 1945, when we ended up in a blasted Munich. Here began a friendship with a man older than me that lasted until his death in the '60s back in Cortland, New York.

How to describe Frank Piedigrossi? Physically, a tough, very strong, dark-skinned man. Mentally, a caring, devoted father-figure to his men who worshipped him because he was fair and always in there trying to help them. My job became easy and pleasurable because of Frank. All the things I was responsible for were already pretty much in place, and as long as they were through Frank, I let him run the platoon better than I could.

In no particular order, I was responsible for march order, that our platoon was in proper column, with proper distances between vehicles. I took care of the rations, made out sick call, reviewed all mail to the States, was a watch-dog on ammunition needs, saw to it that pieces were properly dug in, and answered gripes from the enlisted men in the platoon. Frank did a better job than I could have, and we hit it off and became close friends.

The Bofors had two bucket seats and we were constantly on guard, with time trials as to actual firing. Digging in the Bofors when we moved was a tough, dirty job and required every man. In those days from October until December, we didn't move many times because the Allied advance of the infantry 2-4 miles ahead of us had been slowed by lack of gasoline. Most of the gas was going to Montgomery in the north. I remember one move at night when we wound up in a northern French town in Alsace, when after billeting my platoon, Frank and I found a small building in the back of a church and ended up sleeping in our bed rolls spread out inside caskets from a mortuary.

I remember very well Easter Sunday, April 1, 1945. We had been given march order and were crossing the red bridge entering Heidelberg. Two ME-109s came at us out of the east, the planes flying just above the top of the bridge. We got one of them with our machine guns and it hit in a black column into the side of a hill.

Frank's outfit had been in the invasion of Sicily; and for a while had been around Palermo defending our 155 artillery pieces. While near Palermo, he fell in love with a local peasant girl by the name of Pierina, and asked her father for permission to marry her. The father refused and said to him in native Sicilian, "You come back after the war all in one piece and you can marry Pierina in Palermo."

After the war, his outfit was scheduled to go back to the States, and I would be sweating out another six months to a year before I would get to go back. Frank did marry the girl and brought her back to Cortland, New York where they lived in a shotgun house and raised a boy and a girl. Two different times, Sally and I had the pleasure of meeting the family on our antique trips to the east. It was interesting to see their very plain house, with the big kitchen at the back in which sat a large round table with a huge blue covered light over the table. This is where the family spent most of their time. The living room was only used by Pierina for weddings and christenings and funerals, and all the furniture was covered heavily with plastic. When you came in her house, you had to take your shoes off.

Albert J. Koerts

Flint, Michigan

Excellent workman in his business, long-time Kiwanian, outspoken curmudgeon, big-cigar smoker, a heart as big as a bushel basket, lover of street waifs, extremely difficult to get to know, tough as nails, and a real Dutchman.

I handled the insurance on his business for more than 30 years and it wasn't easy. Back in the 60s when package policies were the vogue, I put a Reliance Insurance Company package on all of his operations on Lewis Street. It was a few days later that a brash young fellow representing the Reliance office from Detroit came up and waded into Al's office early one morning. He said to Ray who was on the desk at the paint and glass retail store, "I need to go across the street and inspect your new metal-working shop." Ray's answer was, "Sir, Mr. Koerts is now up at Lloyd's Coffee Shop a block away and he has left express orders here that no one goes into his new building without his permission. I'd suggest you wait until Mr. Koerts comes back or you go up there and tell him what you need to do." With that, this inspector says, "I am in a hurry—have a lot of calls. I'll just give it a quick once-over." And with that, he walked across the street and entered the new building.

As he did, Al walked out of Lloyd's and saw the man enter his new building. He hurried in his walk down to the main store and said to Ray, "Who in the hell is that in my new building?" And Ray answered, "Some inspector from the insurance company; said he had to look at the new building, and wouldn't wait. I told him to wait for you and he wouldn't listen." With that, Al went upstairs to his cluttered office and got two padlocks. He briskly walked over to the metal-working building across the street and proceeded to padlock the front door and the back door.

The next thing I knew, my office phone rang. I always liked to get down to the office early, ahead of the gang about a half an hour to look over my work schedule. I answered the phone and it was this rube from Reliance. Said he had to break a window to crawl out. I told him what I thought of him, hung up the phone, and it rang again. The caller merely said, "This is

Julius Caesar," which is what Al sometimes called himself when talking to me. He raised some hell with me and then hung up after I tried to apologize.

Another time I remember was at Kiwanis one day at the old Durant Hotel in its heyday. I happened to be seated at the same table with Al, but I wasn't a party to what happened. Al was the reigning Sergeant-at-Arms and always collected fines early in the program. Sterling Lund, a crony of Al's, was at the same table. Later in the program while the speaker was at it, suddenly Al stood up and started a fight with Sterling. He took the tablecloth and pulled it off onto the floor, with dishes, half-eaten food and all. Then he proceeded to chase Sterling out of the room. It was bedlam. A few minutes later, we found Al sitting quietly at another table. The stunt had all be arranged ahead of time because Al didn't like the speaker.

I was at a Buick golf stag at the Flint Golf Club many years ago and as I drove into the parking lot, I couldn't miss the sight of a Buick Roadmaster, the pride of the Buick Motor Company. It sat where everyone had to see it, including a number of high ranking Buick officials from both town and General Motors in Detroit. On it was a large poster with a painting of a lemon and a sign that said, "This is a lemon." This was Al's way of saying he didn't like his car, that it was a dud.

Al was a native of a small coastal town in the Netherlands. With little fanfare he gave the town a remarkable gift: a three-masted sailing schooner.

Another time he went to a Tiger ball game in Detroit with his pal, Bill Gallagher, the Flint Journal photographer. Bill had won the Pulitzer for photography with a picture taken of Adlai Stevenson sitting on the stage at the IMA wearing a shoe with a hole in it. While the two of them were at the gates at Briggs Stadium, Al took a bunch of dollar bills from his pocket and gave them to a number of kids trying to figure a way to get into the game. Al Koerts was a tough one to figure.

Dr. Sheldon C. Woodward

Portola Valley, California

Sheldon "Woody" Woodward, a father, doctor, teacher, naturalist, photographer, and a gentle man who was a friend to many.

Shel moved to Flint in 1932 when his father was named the Director of Welfare for Genesee County. At first, they lived on the north shore of Orrs Point on then-Long Lake near Fenton. Walt Rundles, a boyhood chum, remembers that they were about the same age, around 11, and they tried to fish with bare hooks, not knowing about worms. It's no surprise they didn't catch any fish. This was the time when many families seemed joined together by the little pond on Ellwood Street in Flint, near where the Woodwards resided. This included the Church family, the Mixer family, the Blocks, the Thatchers, and many others. I can remember skating on that pond and it was almost covered with people.

Walt remembered Shel at Pine Lake, the Boy Scout camp near Linden. In their tent was a kid by the name of Parciarelli who used to wake up and say, "Look at my gorgeous body." At one time both Walt and Woody were counselors at the lake under Scoutmaster Frank Ferry, a legend of a man in those days.

Shel grew up in Michigan. He attended Cranbrook School, Wesleyan University, and the University of Michigan Medical School. He was an Army doctor on ships carrying the wounded back to the States from Europe.

After serving in the Army, Shel moved to California in 1951. Over time his practice of pediatrics evolved into adolescent, family, and educational counseling. He started a family counseling program at Menlo Clinic, one of the first of its kind on the Peninsula. Through his active interest in childhood development, he played a big role in the Charles Armstrong School. This was a unique institution for children.

In 1976, Sally and I took our great western trip, leaving Flint and our friends for six months. They gave us a send-off which included a five pound pail of peanut butter. We headed for Santa Fe where I was to teach basic photography at the little St. Catherine's Indian School, and to meet and be squired around for three months of that summer by both Shel and Nancy Woodward. At one time before he left Flint, Shel had worked for Dr. Tuuri. Shel was to join his partners in California founding the first staff pediatric Menlo Medical Clinic.

Those three months with Shel and Nancy became high, high points in our life. Many times Sally and I would reminisce about Santa Fe and those two wonderful people and their four sons.

Shel Woodward was a tremendous lover of the outdoors and a highly respected doctor, as well as a fine, fine photographer. One day that summer Shel and Nancy picked us up in their van and took us east 20 miles to a tiny Indian settlement called Canoncito.

Here was a pretty little mud and brick church with a huge orange-red cross leaning against the entrance. Next to it, below and to the right a foot or two was a tiny cross marking the gravesite of an Indian girl.

It was a beautiful, sunny day, with the rays of the sun hitting the cross. We had a picnic photographing the site. I was working with some new color film and Shel was photographing it in black and white. I thought my work was rather good, and waited to hear from Shel.

It wasn't until later in the year when we were back in Flint that I had a letter from him. He just told it like it happened. He entered an enlargement which he had made in his dark room at home in the annual *Saturday Review of Literature* photography contest. It won first prize. The black and white shot was much like mine in angle and composition, but much more dramatic. Nancy and Shel won a two-week, all expenses tour of the Caribbean. I have often thought of that day and that time with the Woodwards. Back in Portola Valley, Shel continued his work with children and was much loved by all those who came into contact with him.

Woody was an avid landscape photographer who studied with Ansel Adams and David Vestal. He went on to perfect his skills by concentrating on photographing the Coast Range Mountains, Windy Hill, and the open space preserves around Stanford University. He taught photography to students in Portola Valley Schools and held workshops at the Little Red Schoolhouse. He frequently contributed his photographs to the *Country Almanac*. For more than 15 years, Shel volunteered as a docent specializing in botany at Stanford's Jasper Ridge Biological Preserve. He also served on the archives committee of the town of Portola Valley and was the town's official photographer. He and his wife Nancy became docents at Stanford. They took many visitors to Santa Fe, New Mexico during summers. Shel was particularly fond of that area of the country.

I was saddened when he became ill with lung cancer at the age of 72 and passed away. More than 300 people from all walks of life came to Coal Mine Ridge to pay their respects to this great human being. The obituary, which my great friend Woody Block sent me, said, "Woody touched people's lives with all his senses; he didn't just hear, but he listened; he didn't just see, but understood; he asked questions and encouraged others to do the same. The answers were never as important as the questions. He had a quizzical eye. He left a trail of beauty in his place."

After the celebration of his life and all it stood for, the 300 strong walked down the hill together. There was a feeling of life from having joined together. Here was the love and friendship of a charming and inspiring man who lived his life as a splendid adventure and took many people with him.

Jerry H. Rideout

Flint, Michigan

I must agree with Mark Hicks, who wrote a lead local news story in the *Flint Journal* in July 2003, that if there was one thing that Jerry had a passion for, it was writing. I have just come back from visiting Marge, Jerry's wife of 61 years, who now is a spry 90-year old. She said that Jerry was "…a perfectionist. Writing was a gift of his life, and he had a way with words most people do not have."

Jerry had a full, rich life and it was a pleasure to know him, to visit with him at the Flint Golf Club, and to share his many stories and anecdotes about all those people he knew through the years. He passed away at the age of 89, and many of those who knew him will tell you stories about him until the cows come home.

For almost 20 years Jerry headed public relations for the Buick Motor Company and was a key player in developing the Buick Open Golf Tournament, a special place on the PGA tour. Originally a reporter for newspapers in Kentucky and Pennsylvania, he later worked for United Press and became a news editor at Chicago and then the New York Bureau.

As head of public relations for Buick, he was very instrumental in shaping the public's perception of the Flint automaker. To build up the Buick Open in the old days, he persuaded major stars like Perry Como and Andy Williams to attend. In 1987, he was inducted into the Greater Flint Area Sports Hall of Fame for his promotional work for the Buick Open.

In 1964, Jerry was awarded the Silver Anvil by the Public Relations Society of America for creating the *Buick Factory Whistle Show*, a radio program geared toward Buick employees. Jerry also served on the Genesee County Parks and Recreation Commission and was a member of the Flint Golf Club serving as its President, the Flint City Club, and the Hundred Club of Flint.

I personally remember his everlasting passion for golf. On the weekends, he used to get up at 4:00 a.m. on Saturday to go play golf, come back and take his son on the boy's paper route. Then he'd go back to the club and play 18 holes with Marge, his wife.

I remember talking to Jerry once after he and Marge had come back from a trip to China. He was a member of the Circumnavigators Club and had traveled widely. As we sat at the club, Jerry smoking his cigarette and having his usual martini, he said, "A funny thing about the capital city in China. When Marge and I were there, when we woke up in the morning, there were no bird songs, no bird calls, no birds that I could see anywhere. It was very strange. So we asked our guide, and he said there had been an epidemic, a pestilence in the city a year ago, and the city authorities had decided that it had been brought in by the birds. So I asked the guide what had happened then. He said that everyone in each household had to have at least one person all day long banging on dishpans and pans and cans so that there was so much noise that the birds were afraid to alight, and they flew until they fell from exhaustion. After a while, the authorities felt that the pestilence had been eliminated. Then Jerry said to me, "It's just like humans. If you don't keep your feet on the ground, no progress is made."

Whenever I think of Jerry, I think of the Buick Open, the PGA tournament at Warwick Hills in Grand Blanc, just south of Flint. For many years, Jerry WAS the Buick Open, according to Jack Saylor, the writer for the *Detroit Free Press*. I'd agree with him. In Saylor's column, he quoted Jerry who said, "I came to Buick as assistant public relations director—this was 1950. At the time, Chevy had the Soap Box Derby and Fisher Body had its Craftsman model body competition. I was a golf nut—always have been. I kept telling my boss, Waldo McNaught, that 'Buick's gotta get something for identity every year.' "

The breakthrough came in 1958, General Motors 50th anniversary. GM wanted promotions to tie in with the occasion. Rideout got his wish and they started the Buick Open. The purse the first year on the PGA event was a big $52,000, with the winner getting $9,000 and the use of a new Buick every year for five years. Billy Casper won it. (As an aside here, I remember because Casper was a great devotee of fishing, and he caught some bass at one of the local lakes.)

Then Rideout, who replaced McNaught in 1959, had to buck odds almost every year as the Buick went fender-to-fender with the British Open. The old Buick Open died in 1969, on orders from former board chairman Frederic Donner—and it was a low point in Rideout's PR career.

Rideout's favorite Buick Open champion, without question, was Tony Lema, winner at Warwick in 1964 and 1965. Jerry always got a lump in his throat when he spoke fondly of Tony. He was quoted as saying of Tony, "He was just an all-around nice guy. He would do anything for you." One last favor for Rideout ended Lema's life. Lema was in a small plane on a flight to Illinois to play in a Monday-only golf tournament as part of a Buick promotion. The plane crashed, appropriately on a golf course, and Tony was killed.

One day Jerry told us about one year that Arnold Palmer played in the Buick Open and Palmer got up on the stage at Warwick and played drums with the band. . .

When I interviewed Marge, Jerry's lovely wife of 90, she showed me a clipping of an article by Judd Arnett, the *Free Press* writer extraordinaire, who was also one of the many friends and admirers of Jerry. In it Judd said,

> To the astonishment—yeah, the disbelief—of legions of health faddists and medical specialists in general, Jerry Rideout attained his 80th birthday. This miracle was observed at the Bloomfield Hills Country Club and one of those offering a toast said in simple awe, "He has done it by doing everything wrong." He has smoked for at least 60 years and has no intention of quitting; his favorite food is pork chops; and he has finished enough Canadian Club Manhattans to float a 30-foot sailboat bucking a strong headwind. His medicine consists of one aspirin a day and in the flush of the festivities his question was, "Will you do this for me when I'm 90?"

Then Judd added this about Jerry,

> When you thrash your way through all of the chaff, the best of life are those you love, either kin or friends. Of the latter, they fade in and out as your way of life changes, but they return quite often at unexpected moments, especially for the curmudgeon when he has trouble getting to sleep. Then he will quite often recall those with whom he was associated with during the plague of Huns and Japanese; or as golfing partners long ago departed; or as young business strivers after the war who were trying to make the American dream become a reality; or as playmates or schoolmates who have faded into the dimness of many years past. The enemies have been forgotten, at least memory-wise. Only the friends and loved ones remain. Others have such moments, one suspects. After all, it is the best part of life's remarkable slide show.

Jerry, at 82, was interviewed by the *Journal* and this is what part of the article stated, "*Writing:* has had more than 100 letters published. 'I never write a letter unless I have something to bitch about.' *You can tell a Rideout letter by its brevity:* 'I'm an old newspaper man, so I know they like short letters.' *Topic that never fails to spin his top:* 'The anti-smoking hysteria that is sweeping the country.' *Is he a smoker?* 'Hell, yes.'"

A Rideout greatest hit (September 21, 1995): "Now that Michael Moore has become a successful TV movie producer, I wish his glamorous wife would teach him how to dress like one."

Dean Howe, the fine sports writer from the *Journal*, remembers one day when he was sitting in Jerry's living room and Jerry was regaling him with great stories. Jerry told about the day he was sent to Chicago to cover an Illinois vs. Northwestern football game in the 50s. The editors of his paper had asked him to do a piece on Red Grange, the former Illinois All American. Not being versed in American college football history, Rideout said to the man sitting next to him in the press box, "I'm here to do a story on Red Grange. Who in the heck is Red Grange?" The man sitting next to him said, "Me."

Barbara Forker

Green Valley, Arizona

I knew Barbara when she was in my class of 1938 at Flint Northern High School in Flint, Michigan. She had an outstanding record as a woman athlete and was awarded four letters in sports, the highest number given at that time in the school's history. She was a stunning, good-looking and popular young lady in high school. Her record after high school was exemplary.

Beginning after high school, she received a B.S. in 1942 at Eastern Michigan University, an M.S. in 1950 at Iowa State University, and a Ph.D. in 1957 at the University of Michigan in Ann Arbor. By that time she had already been a physical education instructor at Wyandotte, Michigan (both in elementary and high school), a Red Cross girl in the European Theatre in World War II, and from there she climbed a steady ladder of success. I saw her briefly after the war when I was helping to run the Berchtesgaden Hof in Berchtesgaden. She was a Red Cross girl in northern Germany at the time.

Her professional career consisted of Instructor, Assistant Professor, Associate Professor and finally Professor (1957-58) at Iowa State University. From 1958-74 she was Professor and Head of the department of Physical Education for women at Iowa State; Professor and Head of the department of Physical Education and Leisure Studies for both men and women; and from 1978 until 1986, she was the Distinguished Professor and Head of the department of Education and Leisure Studies for all students. This is a remarkable contribution to physical education, and she was one of the first women to hold this last honor at any major university in the United States.

Her honors fill a page of her vitae, including:

- Professor of the Year at Iowa State University (1963)
- Fellow of the American Academy of Kinesiology and Physical Education (1974)
- Distinguished Fellow award at her own high school in Flint (1986)

- One of the first five ever honored at the Education Alumni Hall of Fame at Eastern Michigan University.

In biographical listings, it must be mentioned that she was listed in

- *Who's Who in American Women*
- *Personalities of America*
- *Community Leaders of America*
- *The Two Thousand Women of Achievement*
- *Foremost Women of the Twentieth Century*.

In addition to her many achievements, it is only fair to mention she was a member of

- Governor's Council on Physical Education
- President's Commission on Olympic Sports
- U.S. Olympic Committee Executive Board (1980-84)

Barbara made several speeches to international audiences through the years, including the countries of Indonesia, Iran, Mexico, Greece, Taiwan, the Philippines, and Newfoundland.

In addition to her many professional honors and engagements, those that have had the pleasure of knowing her have all agreed that here is a dedicated, tenacious, loving, marvelous individual, one who has made her old home town extremely proud of her. Her energy and spirit live on in a well-deserved retirement in sunny Arizona.

Bill Billings

Edmund, Washington

Here is a remarkable story.

I first knew Bill when he came from Longfellow Junior High to old Flint Northern High in 1936. I progressed to Northern from Emerson Junior High. I don't remember the first time we met, but we have been close friends ever since. Bill was a natural in sports. His specialty was baseball, which he had played since he was a small boy with his dad and grandfather on their farm northeast of Flint. At Northern he excelled in baseball and won many games for the school as a pitcher. He threw what he called his "junk" pitch. Then when he went to Michigan State University in East Lansing, he was on the team for three years and won many games.

What I remember was the time his friend, Don Mooers (who was the captain of the tennis team at Northern), invited Bill to play tennis for the first time at the tennis courts north of Haskell Community House. Don gave Bill a racket and they volleyed a little because Bill had never played tennis. Then they started.

Bill Billings beat Don at tennis. Don tried to get Bill to join the tennis squad, but Bill was too busy with baseball. Later, as a grandfather, Bill coached baseball for many years.

Bill had a good friend, Mordecai Finkelstein. (Mordecai, incidentally, changed his name to Murray Finley later in life. He became the president of the Garment Workers Union in New York City, a well known union, and he was much admired by all who knew its history.) Bill and Mordecai began to play ping-pong, now known as table tennis. Before you knew it, they were winning the city titles in both singles and doubles.

Now for the clincher. It is 2003 in the state of Washington where Bill now resides. He has been diagnosed with Alzheimer's disease. He and a buddy, Glen Werner, enter the Washington state Senior Olympics in the 80-84 age bracket. Bill wins the gold medal in the singles of table tennis. He and Glen Werner win the doubles.

In 2004 Bill got a silver medal in the sport, which now includes the state of Oregon. He was a great grandpa. How's that for a story?

Thomas Johnson

Bloomfield Hills, Michigan

No one in my lifetime has impressed me more with his wit, his outgoing pleasure in life, and his love for his great family. Tom Johnson is an original, no question.

I first met him at the old Flint Junior College in '39. He was on the basketball team along with other friends of mine including Max Vorce, Bob Timyan, Les Root, and "Red" Dean. Tom was a natural athlete, very impressive and fun-loving, known as "Big Tom." The coach was Charlie Trumbull and he had a bunch of engaging personalities who could also play a fine basketball.

I enjoyed the outline Tom sent me of his life and reprint many of the highlights.

Born in 1917 in Ferndale, Michigan. Attended St. James School on Woodward Avenue where he fell in love in the third grade with Nora Egan, but she wouldn't let him carry her books home. Moved to Flint in 1925 and his father, like most men at that time, went to work for Buick Motor Co.

Tom, a good Catholic, attended St. Mary's High School on the east side. He was captain and center on the Saginaw Valley basketball six-team conference. On graduation, he played basketball for Buick Motor Co. in the old building downtown across from the now-defunct Durant Hotel. At one time, he played a memorable game against the Harlem Globe Trotters where he guarded the famous Tarzan Cooper and each man scored eight points.

He attended the University of Detroit where he had his tuition paid for by playing football. He was coached at the time by the man who instigated the forward pass at Notre Dame. He later tried out for basketball at Villanova where he won a scholarship but it was promptly negated when the coach was fired two weeks later.

World War II began and Tom married one of the loveliest girls in Flint, Betty Ann Olson. He enlisted in the Air Force and became a 2nd Lieutenant, shipped to England on a cruise ship where his roommate was Johnny Lujack, quarterback for Notre Dame and future All-American. Upon arriving in England, he flew one mission with a ceiling at 50 feet.

When the war was over, he had to fly to Lynz, Austria to pick up a number of French prisoners and fly them to some place 60 miles north of Paris. Tom found out that the navigator had screwed up and they were headed out into the Bay of Biscaye. After flying four hours all radio communications were lost and they were running out of gas. He told the navigator that if they didn't land soon, he'd throw him out. At 7:30 p.m., flying on fumes, they spotted an airstrip with two German JU88 fighter planes parked off to the side. Tom put the plane down on a small runway with the outboard engine out of gas. They spotted a white flag and learned the French had captured the field from the Germans just a week before. They could only get 100 gallons of gas, so they made it to a British airfield where they left the French prisoners, flew and got gas, went back and picked up the prisoners and delivered them safely. Then they went back to their base.

After the war, Tom flew a B-17 home via the Azores. It was an unusual experience in that the wings were moving up and down three feet in each direction.

Finally at home, Tom went to work for Traub Manufacturing in the diamond business and became a sales manager. Then an opportunity came along to buy a very fine diamond firm in Chicago, Illinois called Milhening. Here he almost went broke. He was helped by Bob Bellairs and C. J. Miner, Flint folks who were highly regarded. Tom was highly successful with this company until 1984 when he went in a new direction. The business of manufacturing plant equipment fascinated him and he and his son became manufacturer reps for four paint lines.

But, as Tom said many times, his great stroke of good fortune was to marry Betty Ann. Their wonderful marriage produced eight children, all girls except Tom Jr. Tom always said, "I don't care how many zeroes a man has in his bank account. If your kids don't love you, you're a st-----g failure!"

Harriet Kenworthy

Flint, Michigan

Sometime in 1995 an article appeared in *On the Town*, a local magazine, about Harriet. It was like discovering for the first time the real meaning of the two words *community volunteer*. In my lifetime in Flint, there hasn't been a woman more dedicated to her unpaid work, her unofficial trade, than Harriet Kenworthy.

Many years ago, her husband-to-be Watson (about whom a book could be written), was taken off his feet by this tall, graceful lady who came to Flint. The rest is history.

Harriet came from a small farming community in Minnesota, majored in Sociology at Grinnell College in Iowa, and obtained a Master of Social Work from the University of Minnesota. While in college, she whet her interest in Human Services when she worked at a YMCA summer camp for handicapped children from inner-city Chicago. As she said, "I was moved and inspired by their physical accomplishments and their social and emotional growth."

In Flint, she enjoyed the charitable service role of the Flint Junior League. Wherever you go in the community of Flint, you find the influence of Harriet, an influence that is steady, quiet, firm, positive, and charming.

Today Harriet is a sustaining member of the Junior League, having served as its president. The list of organizations she has contributed her time to is legion, including the Flint Community Schools, Child Welfare Society, YWCA, Community Foundation of Greater Flint, McLaren Regional Medical Center, and the Foundation for Mott Community College.

Her honors include a building named for her in downtown Flint because of her untiring efforts with the Genesee County Mental Health Services. Other honors include Honorary Marshall for Commencement Exercises at Grinnell College, Social Worker of the Year award, Liberty Bell award from the Genesee County Bar Association, and the Outstanding Volunteer award from the National Association of Fundraising Executives.

This doesn't tell the story, doesn't present the human side, the love for people, the dedication to people, service far beyond board memberships and responsibilities. So I interviewed Harriet, hoping to shed some light on her great career as a volunteer, and this developed:

PJB: Harriet, your life is so interwoven with volunteerism, it's hard to put the facts down so as not to bore the reader. Can you shed some light?

HK: Sure. Let's start with the YW. In my senior year in college, I served as its president. It was also my first stop when I arrived in Flint in '52. My mother always told me that if I ever found myself in a strange city, the Y was the place to go. It was an inexpensive, friendly answer for me.

PJB: The Y was your stepping stone?

HK: Yes. In those days, most all the community leaders were men. No women then in Flint served as chair of a board and never as a member of a finance committee.

PJB: Were you a wave-maker?

HK: No. But my skills were tested during my Y presidency. In the early 70s, our national Y had voted to accept the one imperative, "To thrust our collective power toward the elimination of racism wherever it exists and by any means necessary." It was a very bold statement and it came at a time of great racial unrest. Institutional racism was a new concept and we had to do a lot of soul searching and self-examination. It was a time of great struggle throughout the country and there was much tension. And also, Phil, there was much increasing emphasis on the YWCA as a woman's movement, with women embracing "women's lib." I had just accepted Co-Chair of a YWCA $2.5 million Directions 90 capital campaign, and I had no record to go on as a fundraiser. I believed in the cause and it was successful. I found that I could do something that I didn't know I could. So a lot was going on at the Flint Y and I was right in the middle of it.

PJB: You've been involved for many years with Genesee County Mental Health.

HK: I remember how President Kennedy asked for a broad new approach to using federal dollars. Large institutional care to be replaced by community prevention, treatment and rehab services. I was on the first Mental Health board. This was a very dramatic shift in the way services were provided. We could see improved access to care for a great many people in a more humane manner than in state hospitals. I also remember many strenuous exchanges with state and county officials over funding.

PJB: What about McLaren Regional Medical Center [then McLaren Hospital] and your activity there?

HK: Enormous changes took place in the delivery of health care. Here came escalating health care costs, a massive shift in financing, huge technical advances, much competition between health care institutions—many ethical issues—all very fascinating.

I'd like to speak of Priority Children.

PJB: I'm acquainted because of my years on the board at Mott Children's.

HK: Here we're trying to improve the life of children and families, and it's very unsettling with all of the problems today…children living in poverty, born to single parents, teen pregnancies, child abuse, school drop-outs, being raised by their grandparents, those living in foster care. You know, we keep throwing money away putting out fires and dealing with problems after they become emergencies. I realize the return on investment in prevention is very high, and when money is tight, prevention programs are the first to be cut, and yet they are so terribly important. Here, Phil, I want to mention the Child Welfare Society. Before I joined their board, it operated a home for children referred by the Probate court. When foster care became the preferred way of caring for children who couldn't live in their own homes, we reopened as a day care center. There was a long waiting list and we thrived and United Way was very supportive. Then came societal shifts; like the way the state made reimbursement for child care. There came a decrease in United Way support. We do now have, fortunately, an alliance with Mott Children's Health Center which promises a new and exciting chapter for us.

PJB: You haven't mentioned United Way.

HK: United Way has reflected the enormous changes in the downward economy of Genesee County. From a successful campaign of over $9 million in 1986-87 when employment was at its peak, we're now struggling to raise $5 million. We've had to adopt many more ways to allocate the dwindling resources.

PJB: And your recent term on the Flint Board of Education, Harriet?

HK: I witnessed terrible dissension there and a very troubling lack of focus. At least they've finally come to work together with the important issues. It was a very demanding experience for me.

PJB: Some concluding thoughts?

HK: Well, my self-identity continues as a social worker. While the mission of a particular agency determines what social workers do, the profession of social work still determines how it is done. It certainly deepens your understanding of human worth and dignity and provides the ethical framework.

My volunteerism has stretched my mind and my learning. I've been enriched by knowing people whose life situations are different than mine, whose boundaries and values are different.

It's been highly satisfying working for things that are important.

Woodrow "Woody" Skaff

Flint, Michigan

I first bumped into Woody after World War II when I attended a Junior Chamber meeting at the Home Dairy on Kearsley Street and Joe Ryder was speaking. Both Woody and I were so impressed that we signed up with Joe that night to become Big Brothers. We took on boys to help. Woody was starting a carpet and furniture operation on Harrison Street and Joe had finagled him into employing on a part-time basis some of the boys we helped. I have heard Woody say that at one time, he had at least ten boys employed.

In those days after the war (1946), I was running around trying to sell insurance, working ten hour days and driving my wife nuts. All the while she was feeding Steve, our first born, and pregnant with Laurel. My father was in the early stages of Parkinson's disease and needed help badly (personnel-wise, for sales calls). One of my early calls was on Woody. I was able to see what insurance he carried and mentioned that he'd be wise to have a reporting form of fire insurance, so that at all times he would have top dollar coverage on all of his inventory and would only be paying for what he had. His specific amount of coverage didn't give him what he needed when his inventory rose, and when it was low, he had too much. I convinced him and he found out in a hurry. A few months later, he had a whopper of a fire (at that time he was having union problems and worried that maybe that was the cause of the fire). Nothing ever came of it, though. I saved him a lot of money with the insurance I recommended.

A little later, I recommended business interruption insurance to protect his earnings as well as inventory and again he had a fire. From that day on, my firm did business with him—and still does on the big operation out on Hill Road. So that's over 55 years of service on that account, way after I retired.

I had first heard of Woody at Flint Central because he was a forward on their basketball team and had what they called "soft hands." He was an outstanding player for Central.

An outstanding businessman, he has spent much of his time since retirement volunteering for First Presbyterian Church. He calls on "shut-ins," people who are unable to leave their residences but appreciate Woody and the time he spends with them. To me he has always been known as "Smiley" because of his happy disposition.

His list of community affiliations is like a Who's Who, including the Flint YMCA, Big Brothers, NBD Bank, Downtown Optimist Club, and the Flint Rotary Club. Recently he was named a Distinguished Fellow by the Central High School Alumni Association and given the same honor by Mott College. In 1952 he was named "Man of the Year" by the Flint Junior Chamber of Commerce.

One of his proudest achievements was to bring Young Life, a Christian organization for young people, to the Flint area in the 60s. Many local young people have had life-changing experiences for the better that would not have been possible without Woody's initiative.

But I must tell a story because I was part of it and I have told it many times in Flint. It might have been either in the 50s or 60s. It was when Bill Bishop had his Allsports store down on First Street. One time in the early summer, Joe Ryder and I decided that Woody had to learn how to fly fish. First, Joe took Woody up on the Tobacco River near Clare to teach him how to fish. I wasn't along that day and wished I had seen what happened.

He got Woody in the river with an old pair of waders and a second-hand fly rod—all part of Joe's beaten down equipment. Then he tried to show Woody how to throw the line. There luckily wasn't any fly attached to the line because a game warden came along and tried to give Woody a ticket because he didn't even have a license. Joe was able to talk the warden out of it.

Then one day Joe called me and we took Woody down to Allsports and really outfitted him. I think the bill was over $500. That was alright with Woody, but somehow Margaret (his wife) saw the bill and raised hell with Woody. Then one early summer day, a gang of us went up to fish the Maple between Brutus and Pellston, and stayed in some log cabins at Alanson. There were Woody, Joe, Tom Purdy, Cy Lewis, Rex Graff, and me. Woody met us with his own car. We decided that Joe and I would put Woody in at the iron bridge south of Pellston. Here there was a good run under the bridge and there was the possibility that he could catch a fish or two. The day was cold and windy, not a good trout day. We got Woody in the stream with his fancy creel and English reel and a bunch of flies that we tied on some leaders for him. He then had a license and if he got tired, could leave in his car and go back to Alanson.

Joe and I left him and said we'd be back about 5:00. We picked out sections of the stream north of him toward Pellston and had a very poor day on the stream, insofar as catching brookies or an occasional brown. But just being on the little stream itself was great. I had fished it since I was eight and I loved its pools and cut-banks and an occasional deer that would come to drink. Eventually we went back to see how Woody had fared, knowing it was a waste of his time. Lo and behold, Woody met us with his patented smile and opened his creel to show us four beautiful rainbows all about 12-inches. He had caught them all under the bridge.

That night after supper, with everyone being pretty skunked except Woody, we started to play poker. Woody sneezed and pulled a handkerchief out of his pocket. Out came a slip of paper that floated down to the floor. I picked it up and it was a receipt for four rainbows from the Ottawa Trout Ponds, just north of Alanson.

Cliff Drury

Lansing, Michigan

On Torch Lake in northern Michigan is a camp known affectionately as Hayo-went-ha. It is a YMCA camp and over the years thousands of boys have enjoyed it. It has an enviable record of service and is known as one of the finest camps in the country. Much of this reputation is the work of one man, Cliff M. "Cap" Drury. Cap was the director for 36 years. He affected many lives for the good. When he finally retired, he found himself appointed as a special World Service Director in Japan and, due to his untiring efforts, was instrumental in the development of an international camp in Hokkaido known as Camp Chimikepp. He was so loved over there that the Japanese government gave him their highest medal for service available to a non-Japanese.

When I think of "Cap," I remember one time early in the spring of a year long ago when the ice was still in old Torch Lake. He put the docks in all by himself because they had to be put in and there wasn't anyone else around to do it.

Cap wrote a Christmas message each year to his boys of that previous summer and I reprint it here.

I Am the Tall White Pine

The rather lonely giant that stands along the path on the way to Buell Chapel

I have stood there for a good many years . . . long before the friendly acres round about became a happy vacation land for boys.

And tonight . . . I am a little more lonely than usual because of a softly falling snow that is keeping most of the forest creatures home.

Oh yes, Old Torch moves restlessly here at my feet and there is the company of many other trees.

But still I'm lonely . . . thinking about and longing for the return of that happy multitude whose joyous shouts and rompings I have been accustomed to look for each summer.

At times I wonder where all those boys are . . . wonder if they, too, had grown as did that Boy some 20 centuries ago "in wisdom and stature, and in favor with God and man."

Oft times I wonder if each of these boys these past 60 years realizes there has been much sacrifice on his behalf, that each might achieve his best, even as I.

And long ago, that Boy, grown to manhood, was compelled to lug one of my kind, fashioned into a crude cross, to the top of a hill called Calvary

because of his beliefs that we today accept and cherish.

And was he not called the Prince of Peace?

In this forest loneliness there seems to be peace. But I am doubly sure of it when I see these lively youngsters playing, singing, and living together on this beloved acreage that is Hayo-went-ha.

Tonight my branches heavy with snow and with the spirit of Christmas in the air, I should like to speak for all that which makes our camp, wishing you

> Joyous Season's Greetings and a
> sincere wish to that you may return to my
> summer's shade.
>
> Clifton "Cap" Drury

Arthur L. Tuuri, M.D.

Flushing, Michigan

Back in 1967, almost 40 years ago, there appeared in our *Flint Journal* a full page article on the crown jewel in Flint, the Mott Children's Health Center, located adjacent to Hurley Hospital. I had the pleasure of being a board member there for almost 25 years until I retired from the insurance business and Sally and I moved to Florida.

I had the occasion to serve under its director, Art Tuuri. For my money, he was the finest individual I ever had the pleasure of knowing.

In the *Journal* article I refer to, there are comments from several people about this man, and I mention them below.

From Elizabeth Conway and Dolores Fialka (Elizabeth was the *Journal* staff writer and Dolores was Dr. Tuuri's assistant for 25 years). Here's what they agreed on:

"Dr. Tuuri is perhaps one of the quietest, most sensitive and humble men in Flint, so he finds it difficult to accept the credit that is given him by thousands of affectionate parents, as well as his associates, civic leaders, and those in the dental and medical fields."

C. S. Mott wrote in his diary under the date of 2/15/55, just before Dr. Tuuri left for service and the Army, "He is undoubtedly the finest head of our health operation that we have ever had or could ever get."

Frank J. Manley, executive director of the Mott Foundation, said, "The center is a monument to a dedicated humanitarian."

Milton Sacks, administrator of Hurley Hospital: "It is more than coincidence that the pediatric services at Hurley and Mott Children's Center have demonstrated parallel and progressive growth. It is a matter of purposeful alliance and cooperation made possible by the magnificent presence of Arthur L. Tuuri."

It is interesting to me that the premise of the Mott Children's Clinic is this statement: "We approach all problems of children with affection. Theirs is the province of joy and good humor. They are the most wholesome part of the race for they are the freshest from the hands of God."

The clinic, or center, the dream of both Dr. Tuuri and Mr. Mott, focuses on eight areas of child health. This is a far cry from the treatment in Flint during the Depression years. Here is a brief run-down of the center:

Medical – All illnesses of children are treated. A special clinic for skin problems is the latest addition.

Dental – Routine dentistry is provided. Specialized services for physically, mentally, and emotionally handicapped children, and those with cleft palates are available.

Speech and hearing – Hearing testing, speech and language evaluation, and programs in speech and language therapy.

Special education – for disturbed and handicapped children.

Psychiatric – Evaluation and treatment of emotionally disturbed children.

Maternal and infant health – The center considers the child even before he is born. It conducts classes for expectant parents.

Unwed parent counseling – Education in prenatal care and postnatal care and consultation with both the girl and the baby's father are offered.

Social services – Providing leadership in health education.

As Art Tuuri said to us at a board meeting, "The total child health concept gave us stimulus for projected progress. This is because many health, medical-related and educational groups must work together to develop and plan programs to meet the total needs of the child. Each of these groups has a part to play in bringing about the wellbeing and happiness of the child. One group cannot do it alone."

All that center has done under Dr. Tuuri for the thousands of Flint and Genesee County children cannot be measured, except that the expressions of thanks are heard every day. There are no fees charged at the clinic, which is open to all children.

This last statement of Art Tuuri sums it up well:

In each of us exists the limitations and expansions of the world. We pick and choose, make decisions, acknowledge our liabilities and utilize our assets. To each his own, for we are all different. Our parents endowed us with our appearance, but we ourselves direct ourselves, make of our lives what we will.

In our present society almost anything is possible. Education is available to those who strive for it. Career opportunities are panoramic in scope. None should be denied what he is willing to work toward. But one thing is a hindrance. One factor more than any other waylays our high ambitions: poor health.

One who is physically handicapped has a multitude of helpful hands to give direction toward a more productive life; but what of the one with a less obvious health problem? And what of the child who is defeated by health problems before he begins? What a waste to the individual—an equal waste to society.

Life is to be lived! Good health is the vehicle for the journey.

Dr. Tuuri's hemophiliac patients were very special to him and he took them hunting with him right up to the last hunting season before he died. Those kids, many of whom continued going with him as adults, never could have done those things without him.

Current president of Mott Children's Health Center, Roy E. Peterson, said of Tuuri, "He was loved by children, listened to by parents, and respected by people of all ages and levels in the community. He just had that ability to touch people in their hearts and capture their imaginations in the process."

I must refer to the fine obituary that appeared in the *Journal* when Art Tuuri died.

The man who was a champion of children's health care won't be forgotten. His name lives on locally with the Durant-Tuuri-Mott Elementary School in Flint; the Tuuri pediatric wing at Hurley Medical Center; the Tuuri Road Race; and Tuuri Place.

Tuuri was considered a world authority on polio in the 1950s. Most recently, Tuuri worked to secure Community Foundation grants for the development of an AIDS treatment strategy by local health agencies.

Perhaps more telling of his skill and popularity is the fact that some people still call the Genesee County Medical Society seeking a pediatrician "just like Dr. Tuuri," according to executive director Peter A. Levine.

Certainly, no one can replace Arthur Tuuri. Nonetheless, we challenge area physicians and others to be more like him. Our community would be a better place if more people followed Dr. Tuuri's prescription to make it so.

— *from the* Flint Journal *1996*

Bill Lamb

Grand Blanc, Michigan

In one of the forewords to Bill Lamb's book, *The Factory Whistle & Me*, I noted his statement which read, "I am one lucky guy! I got into a profession I loved and though it didn't make me rich, I enjoyed it for 45 wonderful years." This statement I heartily agree with, and have many times repeated this philosophy to those who want sage advice. My point and Bill's is that if you just go into something to make a lot of money, and find that it locks you into something that is distasteful or boring or not to your liking, you are kidding yourself. Probably your resulting life will not be what you wanted it to be. Make sure it's something you love. Work at it.

Bill Lamb, known to some few as Willard, is and was a radio pioneer. He was the first person to broadcast commercially in stereo. He is the one who invented the disc jockey dance concept. He was the first DJ in Flint to broadcast his entire radio program live from his home. He did the *Buick Factory Whistle Show* for 25 years. I would venture to say in that time, he knew more people at Buick Motor Company than the manager or president of the corporation. He was much beloved for his interest, his easy way, and his general attitude toward humanity. He would walk down the assembly line at Buick and many, many of the workers would yell greetings at him because of his respect for them, for the skills they possessed and the car they made, and their kindness toward him.

This from Bob Lamb, a son, "Many nights as we lay in bed we could hear music coming out of the studio downstairs. Dad wrote and produced singing jingles and he would put together small combos and sometimes big bands to create the original commercials. He had salesmen traveling around the country selling his creations to car dealers, department stores, restaurants, etc., and sometimes the sessions would go late into the night or even the morning."

Jeff Lamb, another son, said, "It takes a gifted man to communicate as well as he does. It's a talent to interview a man of Buick who just won a check through the Suggestion Program and make it interesting to everyone. This man may have invented a Langstrom Gangly wrench for use on his specialized machine. This wrench clearly means nothing to other jobs or to the banker or to the sales clerk, but Dad could make that happy man at Buick and his invention interesting to all. Interestingly, the banker, the sales clerks, and the housewives joined the army of listeners to *The Buick Factory Whistle Show* every day for two and a half decades."

You've heard this before, but it is too choice to overlook. When Bill was in World War II in the 40s, he was in electronics school at Chanute Field in Illinois, and you know what happened. They had some WACs and their outhouse was within 50 feet of Bill's barracks. So the men rigged up a speaker under the seat in the ladies' outhouse and when the ladies sat down, a voice would come from under the seat which said, "Excuse me, lady! Could you move over a couple of seats? I'm painting down here." Bill ended up in the MPs overseas in Europe, after all of his radio training, which was typical of the Army.

Back from the service, Bill opened a record shop and played records. He also had a hit program called *Jam for Breakfast*. He started to interview celebrities passing through Flint. That became a real hit with the listeners. While interviewing Frankie Laine who had the records "That's My Desire" and "Mule Train," he inadvertently knocked off Frankie's toupee.

Bill described the time he went to interview Elvis Presley in Detroit: he chartered four Greyhound buses and mentioned that he could take about 150 kids to Olympia Stadium. Tickets were available at his record shop for $6.50, which included bus fare, a box lunch and pop. Among those on board were a doctor, nurse, and policeman. But he never did hear Elvis! When he entered Olympia, the screaming crowd was deafening and the star hadn't even shown up. When Elvis came on stage, the young girls turned up the decibels and his singing just couldn't compete. We saw him. His gyrations suggested an invasion of ants in his wardrobe, but the noise made hearing him impossible. Afterwards, Bill said, "I went backstage and he was sitting yoga style. I interviewed him, but it wasn't a good interview. I didn't ask good questions and he didn't give good replies."

Again, Bill: "Most jingles are good for a few months at most, but we did one for Applegate Chevrolet 25 years ago and they're still using it! It was based upon the national Chevrolet song, 'Baseball, Hotdogs, Apple Pie and Chevrolet.' "

In an interview with the popular Rosemary Clooney, Bill noticed that she looked pregnant. He said to her, "When is the big day?" "What day?" she answered. Bill was so sure he was on solid ground that he asked, "When is the baby due?" There was a pause and she answered, "I am NOT expecting!" With that, Bill turned his recorder off and sat there with his jaw hanging slack. He didn't know what to say. She replied, "That's okay. Don't worry about it." Bill also noted in his book that while Jimmy Dorsey was nice, Tommy was a grouch.

The Factory Whistle Show started in October 1960. In November, Bill met and interviewed Augie Klein, a man working in Factory 36, the engine plant. Augie was Buick's highest seniority employee. He had 50 years in. Augie had started out at Buick as a water boy at age 15, and on that November date, he retired. The next day, Bill met Julius Robinson. Julius had worked in the transmission plant, but before that he had been a carnival worker.

One day Bill was in Factory 25 when one of his mike cables broke which meant no more interviews. One of the people he wanted to interview said, "We can fix that." Fifty feet away was an electrician's crib. They took a hot soldering gun and in about five minutes, Bill was back interviewing Buick employees.

Over the course of the years, Bill did more than 6,000 interviews and became a legend at Buick and in Flint. The funniest story Bill Lamb remembered was told by John Cherveny who was in an outfit fighting the Japanese in the Pacific. In an early assault on an enemy beach, only a few hundred men made it ashore and they were pinned down and asking for heavy gear to help them. Only a few tanks had also come on shore. Finally their pleas were answered and a landing craft hit the shore. When they pulled the heavy equipment off the landing craft, they were dismayed to find that it was a donut making machine.